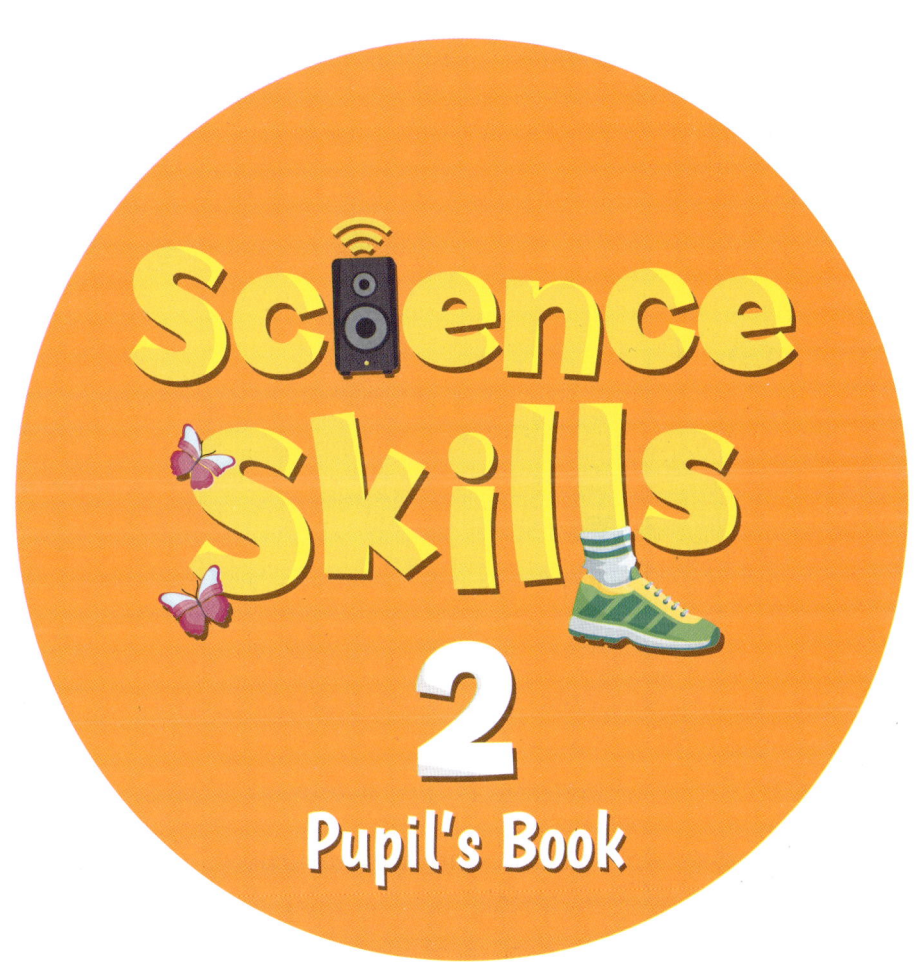

by

Estrella Alarcón   Cristina Domínguez   Berta Quesada

SCIENCE SKILLS 2

Contents

- Introduction to the course characters

Here we go again! — Page 4	
1 Do the locomotion! Motor system — Page 6	• Sections of the body • Bones	• Muscles • Joints
2 An amazing machine Vital functions of human beings — Page 18	• Senses • Digestive System	• Respiratory system • Stages of life
3 All about animals Animals — Page 30	• Mammals • Birds • Fish • Reptiles	• Amphibians • Arthropods • Molluscs
4 All about plants Plants — Page 42	• Trees, bushes and grasses • Wild, cultivated and edible plants • Deciduous and evergreen plants	• Flowering plants • Non-flowering plants: mosses and ferns
5 Building blocks Materials — Page 54	• Natural and non-natural materials • Properties of materials	• House materials • Reversible and irreversible changes
6 Helping me and you Machines — Page 66	• Tools • Simple and complex machines	• Types of energy used by machines • Inventions

Let's review … Page 78

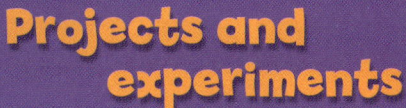

	Projects and experiments		**Mindful time**	**Documentaries**
	• Discover parts of the body. • Make an x-ray.	• Make a muscle. • Make a model hand.	• Remember the beginning.	• Train your muscles
	• Learn about taste. • Make a stomach.	• How much air can you breathe out? • Make a Funny family book.	• Listen to the gong.	• Our senses
	• Discover more mammals. • Make a hanging mobile.	• Animal riddles. • Make animals.	• Be a butterfly.	• Amazing mammals!
	• Make a plant mural. • Make a deciduous tree.	• Make a flap poster for the life cycle of a seed. • Make a class fern.	• We are sunflowers.	• Forever green
	• Make a materials display. • Build a house.	• Learn more about reversible and irreversible changes.	• Different forms	• What is it made of?
	• Make a tool mini book. • Have a race.	• Play a matching game. • Invent a robot.	• Robot massage	• Round and round

Story 1 → Page 90   Story 2 →  Page 92   Story 3 → Page 94

"I can think, predict, experiment, observe and conclude."

Scientific method:
1 Predict
2 Experiment
3 Observe and conclude

Scientist card

Print your finger here when you complete a unit.

Name:

Age:

| Welcome Unit | Unit 1 | Unit 2 | Unit 3 | Unit 4 | Unit 5 | Unit 6 |

the human body

senses

animals

plants

materials

machines

What about you?

My favourite topic is _____ .

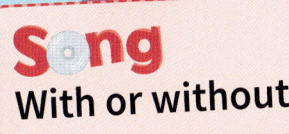

Song
With or without

How can you train your muscles?

Are all the children being careful?

DOCUMENTARY
Train your muscles

WHAT ARE THE LOWER LIMBS?

Label the arms and legs.

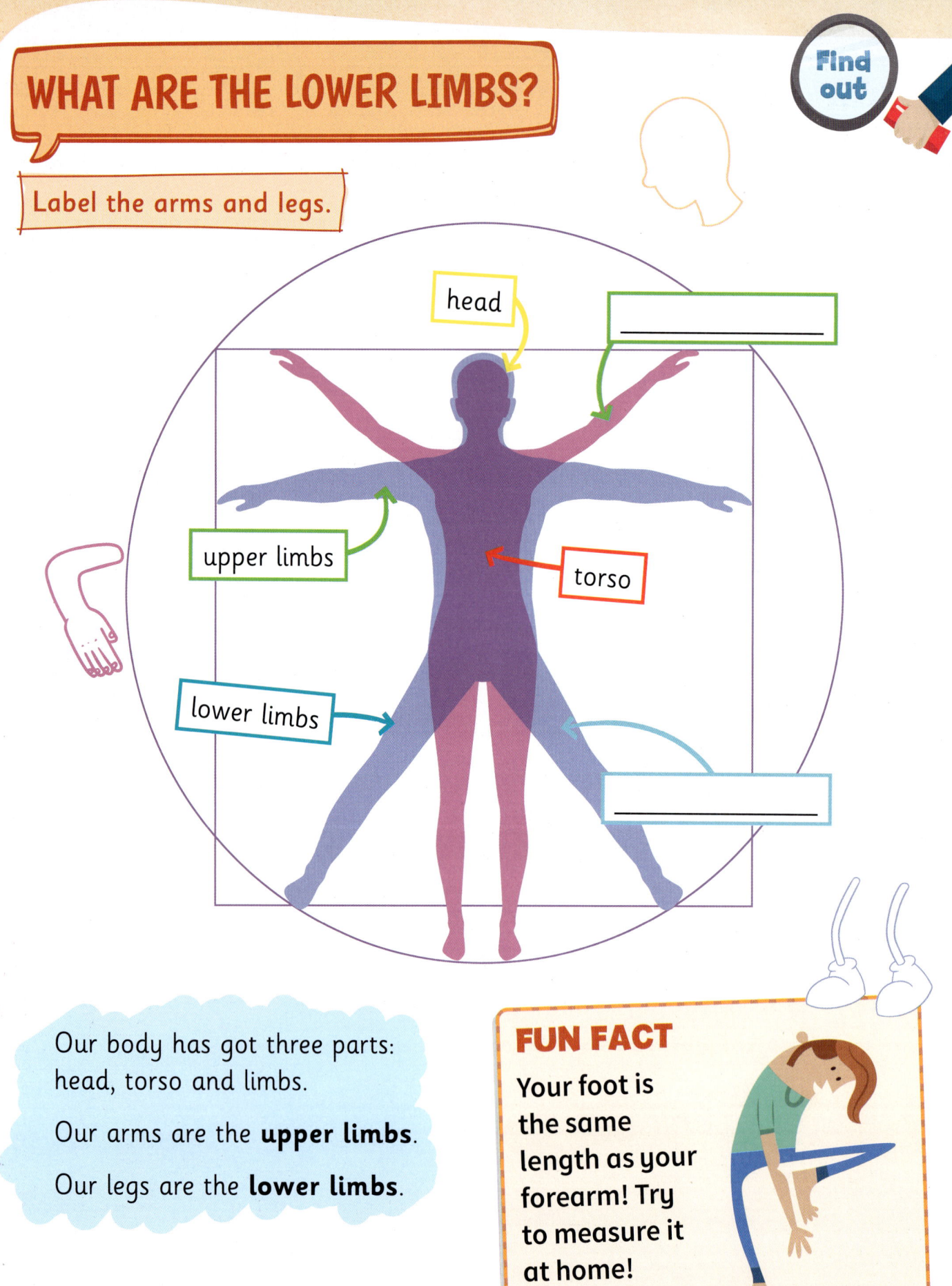

Our body has got three parts: head, torso and limbs.

Our arms are the **upper limbs**.

Our legs are the **lower limbs**.

FUN FACT

Your foot is the same length as your forearm! Try to measure it at home!

Mini-project

Let's discover parts of the body.

1. Work in groups. Choose a friend and draw their outline.

2. Label the body parts.

Show it to your class.

What have I learnt?

My body has got three parts:
h_____ , t_____ and limbs.
My arms are u_____ limbs and my legs are lower l_____ .

MY DICTIONARY

body

head

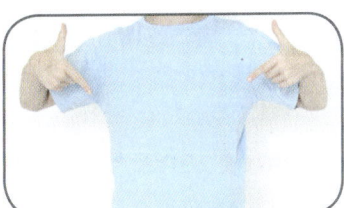
torso

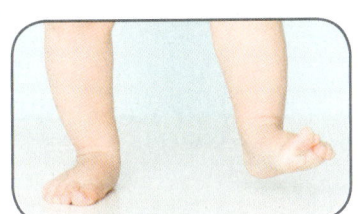
lower limbs

upper limbs

HOW MANY BONES HAVE YOU GOT?

Circle the longest bone.

Our body is made up of bones. Bones are **hard** and **rigid**. They support our body and protect our organs.

Why do we have bones?

- skull
- humerus
- ribs
- pelvis
- backbone
- femur

Can bones break?

Find the skull hidden in the unit!

FUN FACT

There are 54 bones in your hand, fingers and wrist!

Mini-project

Let's make an X-ray!

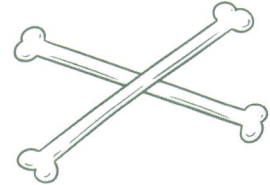

1 Paint the palm of your hand. Press it onto black card.

2 Let the paint dry. Observe your X-ray.

You can try it at home with your foot, too!

What have I learnt?

Bones are hard and rigid. These are some bones in my body:
head bone: s_____
arm bone: h_____
torso bones: r_____ and backbone
leg bone: f_____

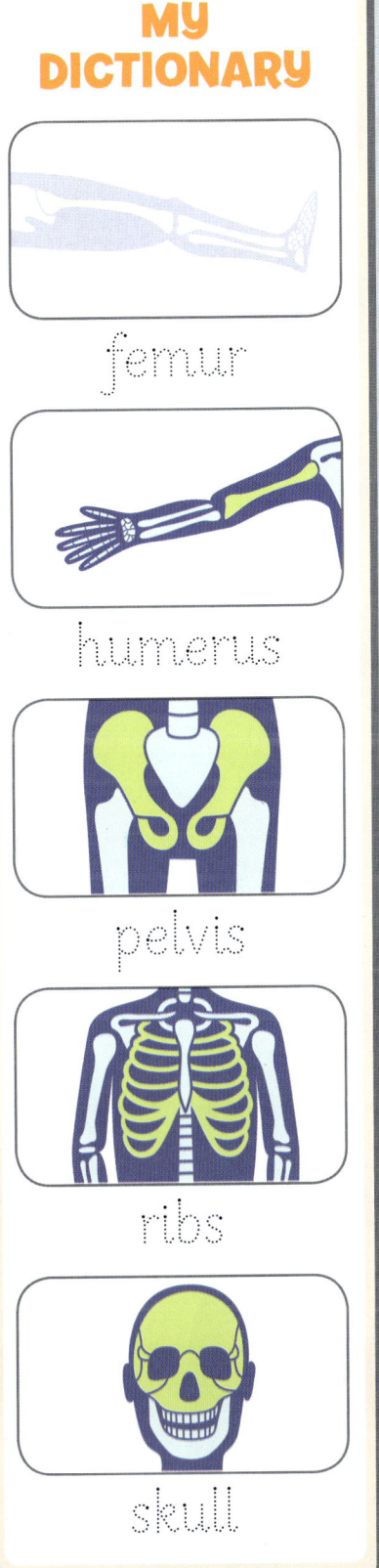

MY DICTIONARY

femur

humerus

pelvis

ribs

skull

HOW DO MUSCLES WORK?

🎧 Listen and point.

Muscles help us move. Muscles are **soft** and **flexible**. They are connected to our bones.

Which is the strongest muscle?

How many muscles have we got?

Muscles can **relax** and **contract**.

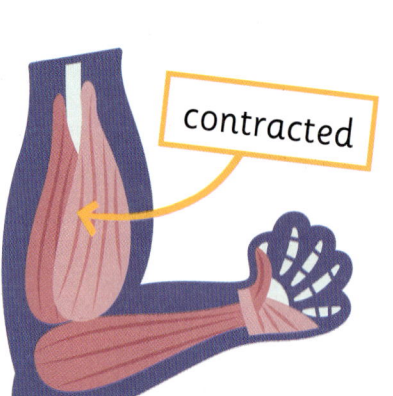

relaxed · contracted

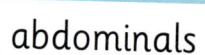

pectorals · abdominals · biceps · gluteus muscles · calf muscles

FUN FACT

Smiling uses 17 face muscles, but frowning uses 43!

Mini-project

> Let's make a muscle!

1 Look at the worksheet. Contract your biceps.

2 Fill in the biceps with plasticine.

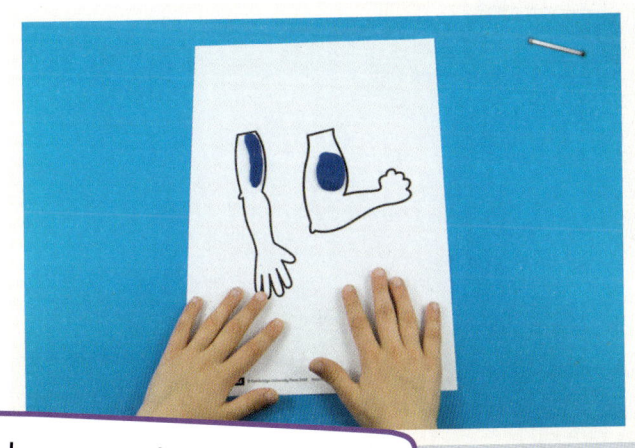

How are they different?

What have I learnt?

Muscles are soft and flexible.
In my torso, I have got p_____ and a_____ .
In my arms, I have got b_____ .
In my legs, I have got g_____ and c_____ muscles.

MY DICTIONARY

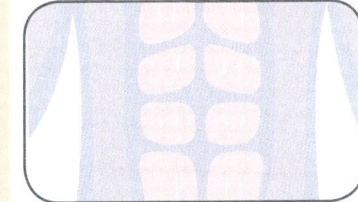
abdominals

biceps

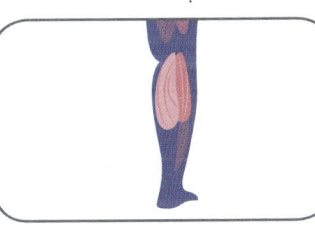
calf muscles

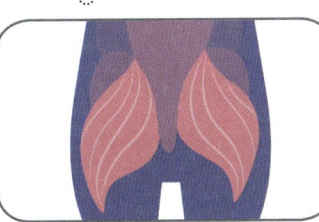
gluteus muscles

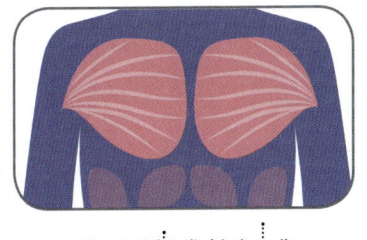
pectorals

WHY DO WE NEED JOINTS?

Circle the joints in the limbs.

Can you move without joints?

Joints connect **bones**. With our joints, we can move and bend our skeleton. Our **muscles** relax and contract when we use our joints.

- jaw
- neck
- shoulder
- elbow
- wrist
- hip
- knee
- ankle

How many joints have we got?

FUN FACT
The jaw is the only joint in the skull that moves!

Mini-project

Let's make a model hand!

1 Cut out a hand. Glue on pieces of a plastic straw.

2 Put cord through the straw. Then, pull the cord to move the hand.

Now you can move the different joints in your hand!

What have I learnt?

Joints connect bones. Some of my joints are the h_____ , e_____ , k_____ , j_____ , and s_____ .

MY DICTIONARY

elbow

hip

jaw

knee

shoulder

Attitude is everything

1 What part of your body do these things protect? Match.

a

b

c

 hands

 knees

 skull

2 Use the words from Activity 1 to complete the sentences.

a

b

c

A helmet protects my _____ .

I wear gloves to protect my _____ .

I have to protect my _____ when I rollerblade.

Now I know

Go to page 78 for more activities.

1 🎧 Listen and write.

a The boy has got a broken _____ .

b The girl on the floor is training her _____ muscles.

c The girl playing basketball is bending her _____ .

2 Draw lines.

humerus

biceps

femur

jaw

abdominals

hip

Chant
Ready, steady, go!

I am Leonardo da Vinci.
I studied the human body. I was a painter, too.
I painted *Vitruvian man*.

17

CAN YOU FEEL IT?

Find something soft in your classroom.

Find out: Different parts of the brain read information from different senses.

We have got five **senses**. The senses connect to our **brain**. We get different **information** from our senses.

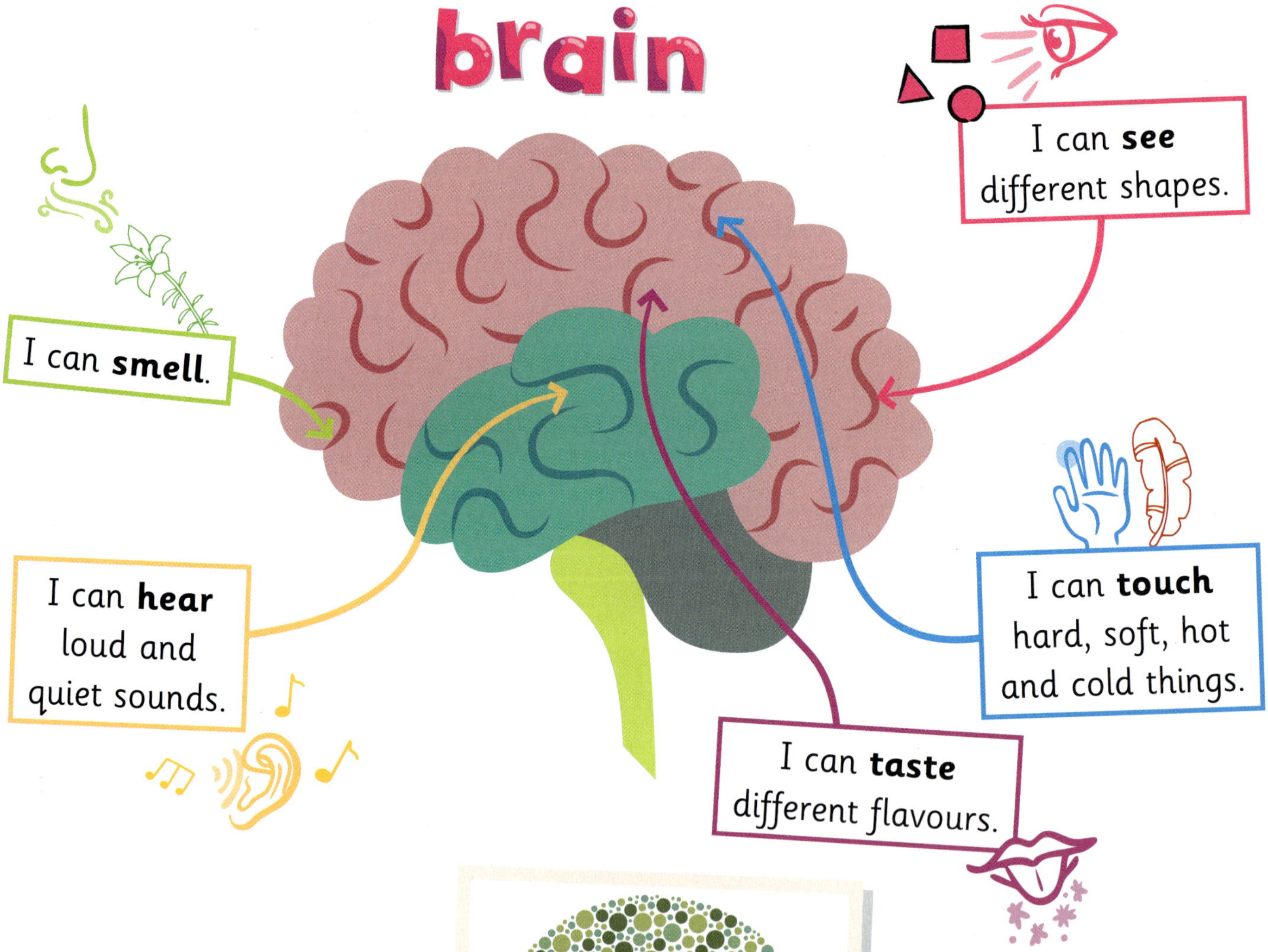

brain

I can **smell**.

I can **see** different shapes.

I can **hear** loud and quiet sounds.

I can **touch** hard, soft, hot and cold things.

I can **taste** different flavours.

Find the feather hidden in the unit!

FUN FACT
Some people are colour-blind. Which number can you see?

> Let's learn about taste.

1 Look at the different ingredients and the key.

salty

sweet

sour

bitter

2 How do you think the ingredients taste? Write.

	Guess!	Yes	No
water and sugar			
grapefruit			
water and salt			
olives			

3 Were you correct? Tick (✓) *Yes* or *No*.

WHERE DOES FOOD GO?

🎧 Listen and number.

We eat, process and expel food through our **digestive system**.

☐ The **small intestine** absorbs the nutrients.

☐ We chew food with our **teeth**.

☐ The **large intestine** takes waste to the anus.

☐ The waste goes out through the **anus**.

☐ The **stomach** breaks the food down into nutrients.

Proteins, carbohydrates and vitamins are types of nutrients.

proteins

carbohydrates

vitamins

FUN FACT
The small intestine is six metres long!

Mini-project

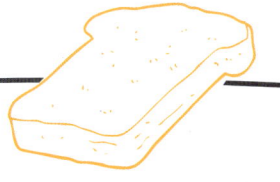

> Try it out

> Let's make a stomach.

1 Take a slice of bread. Break it into small pieces. Put them in a bag.

2 Put three spoonfuls of water in the bag.

> Squeeze it. What happens?

MY DICTIONARY

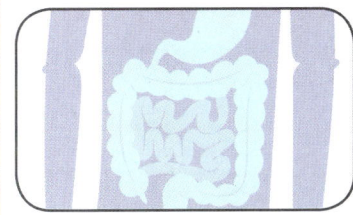
digestive system

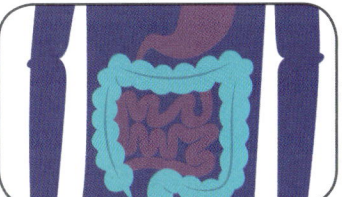
large intestine

small intestine

stomach

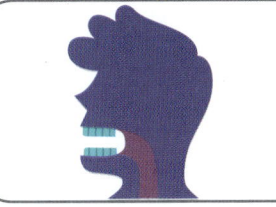
teeth

What have I learnt?

The d_____ s_____
is made up of the mouth, t_____,
s_____, s_____,
i_____, l_____
i_____ and anus.

HOW DO WE BREATHE?

Match the sentences to the picture.

This is our **respiratory system**.

1. We **breathe** in air through our nose or mouth.

2. The air goes to the **lungs**.

3. The **oxygen** goes to the **heart**.

4. The heart pumps **blood** with oxygen around the body.

Find out

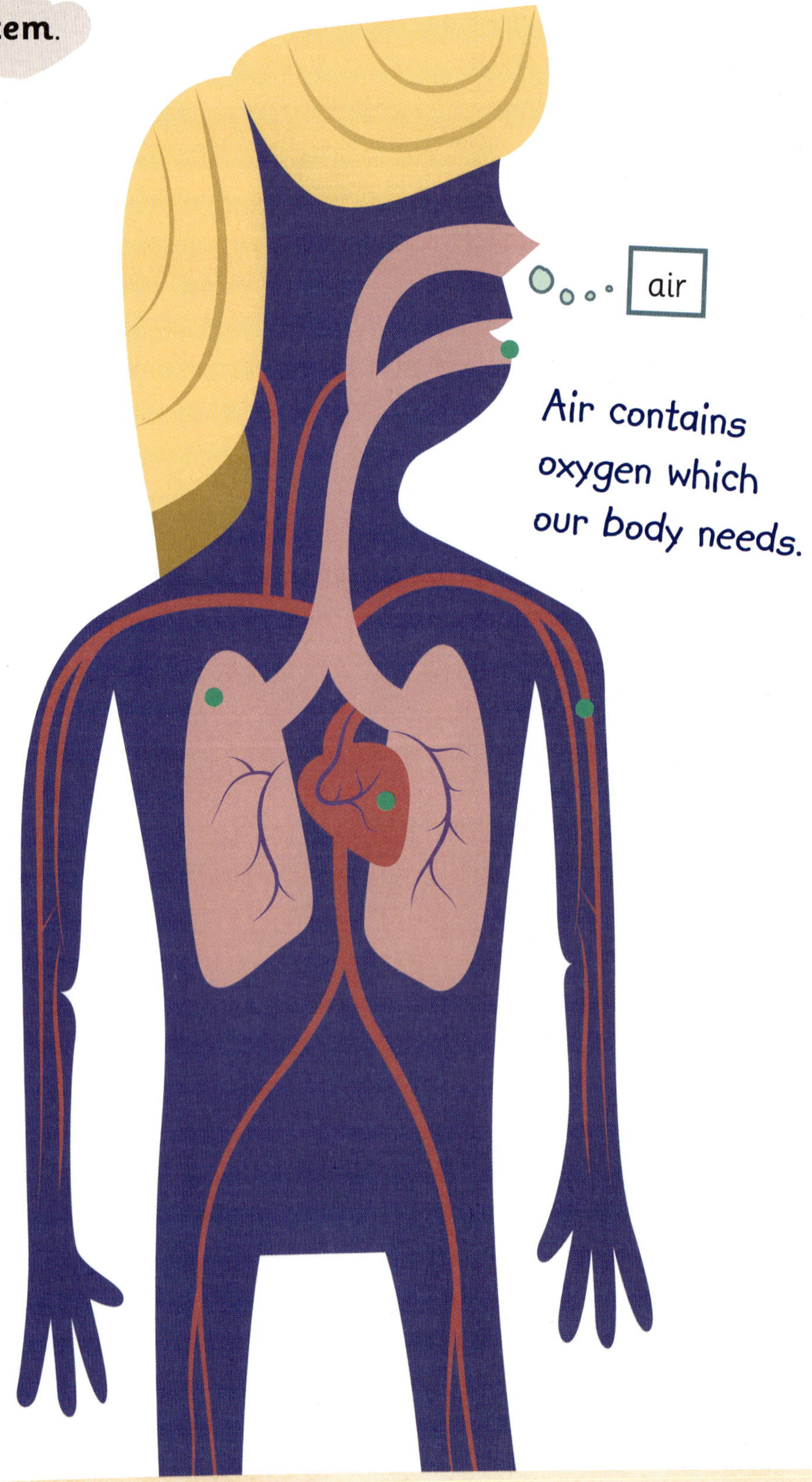

air

Air contains oxygen which our body needs.

Mini-project

> Let's see how much air you can breathe out.

1 Take a deep breath and blow into a balloon.

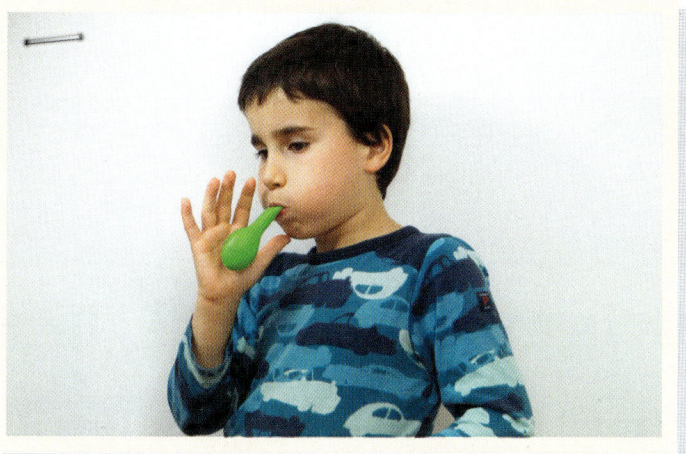

2 Tie your balloon. Compare it to your friends' balloons.

> Who can breathe out the most air?

MY DICTIONARY

blood

heart

lungs

oxygen

Try it out

What have I learnt?

I breathe in air through my nose and mouth. The air travels to my l_____ . The o_____ travels to my h_____ . My heart pumps b_____ and oxygen to the rest of my body.

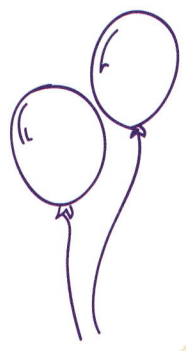

25

ARE YOU GETTING OLDER?

Number the stages of life.

Women have **babies**.

Babies receive **nutrients** and oxygen from the mother's **tummy**.

Babies continue growing after they are **born**.

baby ☐

adolescent ☐

adult ☐

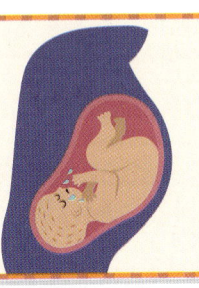
child ☐

elderly person ☐

FUN FACT
Babies cry before they are born!

26

Mini-project

Try it out

Let's make a Funny family book.

1 Colour the family members and cut out your worksheets.

2 Use pins to put your book together. Play with a friend!

What have I learnt?

When I am born, I am a b_____ .
I grow into a c_____ , an ado_____ and finally, an _____ . When I am old, I am an e_____ p_____ .

MY DICTIONARY

baby

child

adolescent

adult

elderly person

Attitude is everything

I can read with my fingers!

1 We have all got special powers. Try these with your friends.

a

b

c

I'm very good at listening.

I'm great at drawing.

I can read a secret message.

2 What is your special power? Draw.

Now I know

Go to page 80 for more activities.

1 🎧 Listen and write the number.

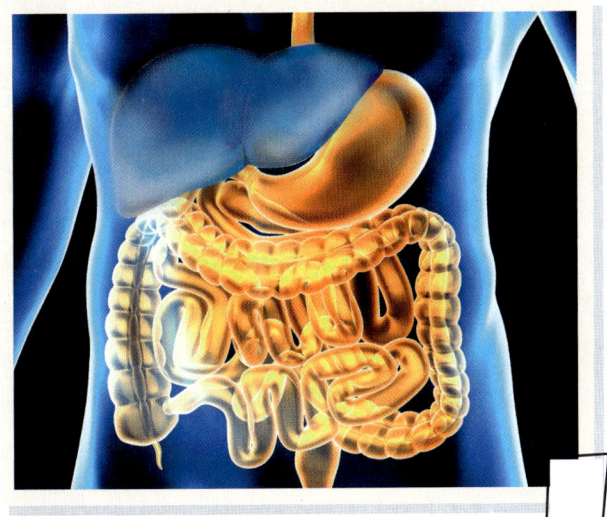
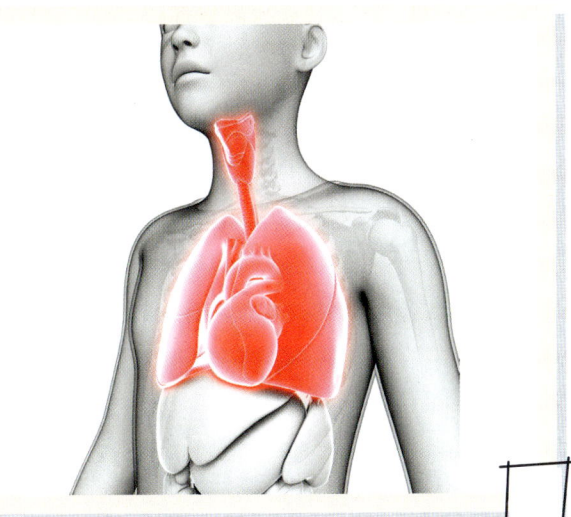

2 Read the text and choose the best answer.

1 What do we use to chew food?
   a the stomach
   b the anus
   c teeth

2 I can smell with my …
   a mouth.
   b nose.
   c ears.

3 My grandmother is …
   a a child.
   b an adult.
   c an elderly person.

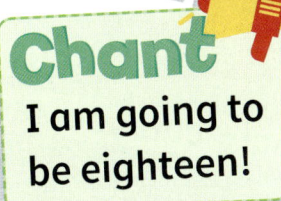

Chant
I am going to be eighteen!

I am Louis Braille.
I invented the Braille alphabet. Blind people can read by touching the paper.

ARE WE MAMMALS?

Draw another mammal.

dog

vertebrates

giraffe

viviparous

lion

hair or fur

Mammals drink milk when they are babies.

Mammals are **carnivores**, **herbivores** or **omnivores**.

How do chimpanzees move?

FUN FACT
Bats have got thumbs.

Find out

Mini-project

Try it out

Let's discover more mammals.

1 Find and cut out photos of mammals. Make a poster.

2 Write about your mammals.

MY DICTIONARY

fur

mammals

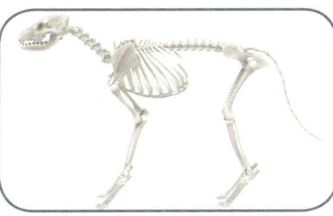
vertebrates

viviparous

What have I learnt?

_____ have got _____ or hair.
They are _____ and their babies drink milk.
They are _____ because they have a backbone.

DO I FLY OR DO I SWIM?

Find out

Circle the eggs.

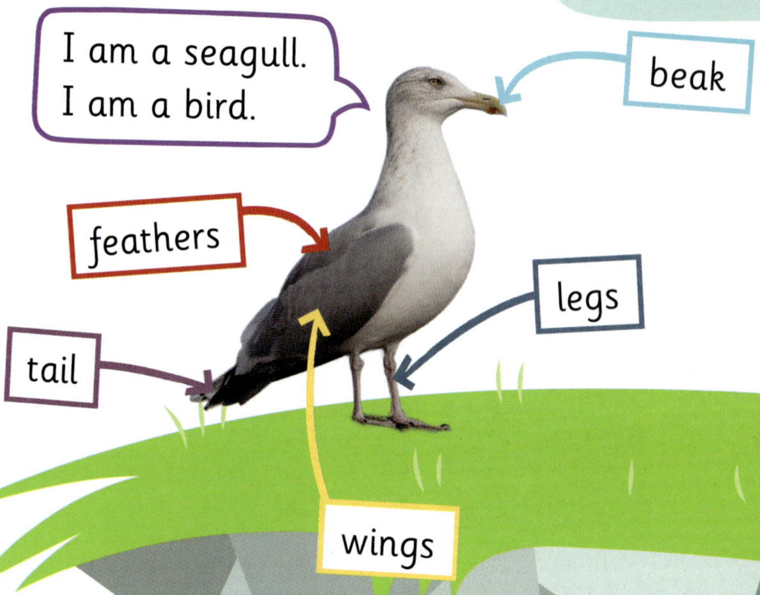
I am a seagull.
I am a bird.
beak
feathers
legs
tail
wings

Birds can be carnivores, herbivores or omnivores.

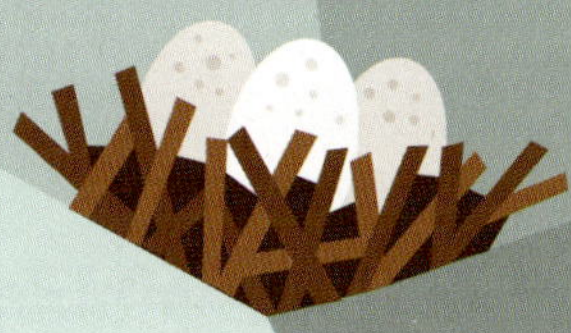

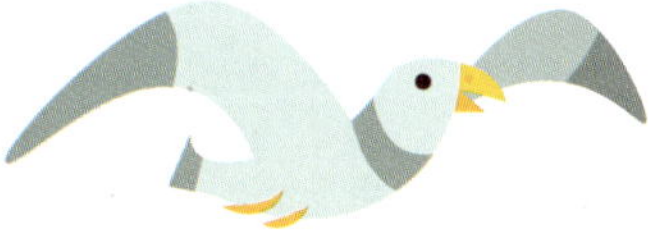

What have birds and fish got in common?

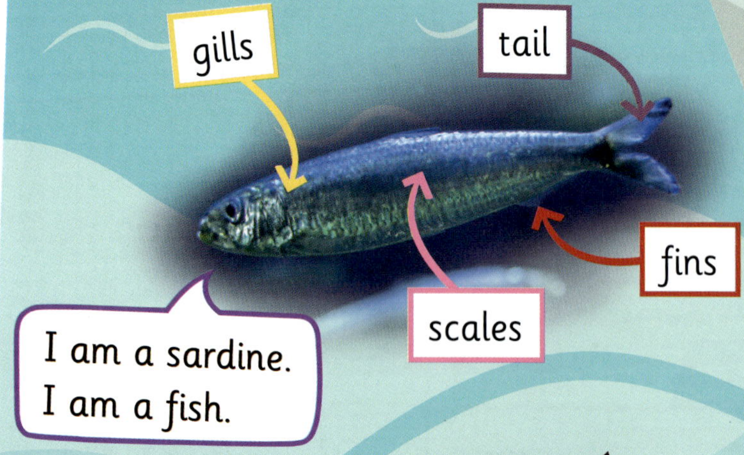
gills
tail
fins
scales
I am a sardine.
I am a fish.

Fish can be carnivores, herbivores or omnivores. Birds and fish are **oviparous**.

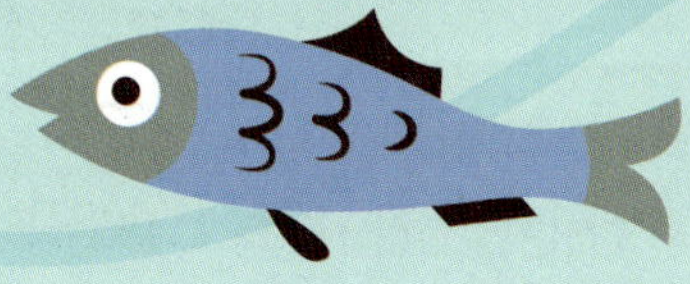

FUN FACT

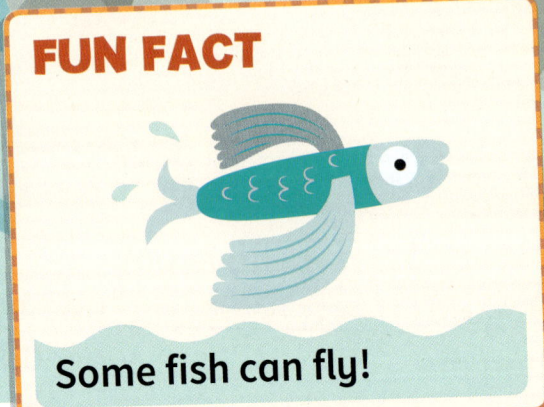

Some fish can fly!

Mini-project

> Let's make a hanging mobile.

1 Colour, cut out and stick the birds to coloured card.

2 Put string through the top of each piece of card. Attach them to pipe cleaners.

Hang your mobile!

What have I learnt?

Birds have got a _____
and _____ .
Fish have got _____
and _____ .
Birds and fish are _____ .

MY DICTIONARY

beak

feathers

fins

gills

oviparous

WHERE DO AMPHIBIANS LIVE?

🎧 Listen and point.

Reptiles and **amphibians** are similar but very different.

Amphibians and reptiles live on **land** and in **water**. They are **oviparous**.

We have got dry skin.

We lay eggs on land.

We breathe with our lungs.

I am a reptile.

We breathe with gills and lungs.

We have got soft, moist skin.

We lay eggs in water.

I am an amphibian.

What do reptiles and amphibians have in common?

Find the hidden butterfly in the unit.

FUN FACT
Snakes replace their skin.

Game Zone

Make riddles with your friends.

1 Cut out photos of animals and glue them onto card.

2 Write clues.

Now play with your friends. Guess the animal!

It's a monkey!

MY DICTIONARY

amphibians

reptiles

dry skin

moist skin

What have I learnt?

_____ have got _____ skin and lay eggs on land. They breathe with lungs.

_____ have got _____ skin and lay eggs in water. They breathe with gills and lungs.

DO ALL MOLLUSCS HAVE TENTACLES?

Trace the words.

Arthropods are invertebrates. They have got **segmented bodies** with limbs and joints.

exoskeleton

tentacles

Molluscs are invertebrates, too. They have got **soft bodies**.

crab

scorpion

snail

octopus

shrimp

grasshopper

antennae

arthropods

mussel

cuttlefish

shell

Where do arthropods and molluscs live?

molluscs

Experiment

Let's make animals.

1 Look at the pictures and talk about them with a friend.

2 Make one vertebrate animal and one invertebrate animal.

What are the main differences between these animals?

Conclusion
What's the main difference between your animals? How do they move?

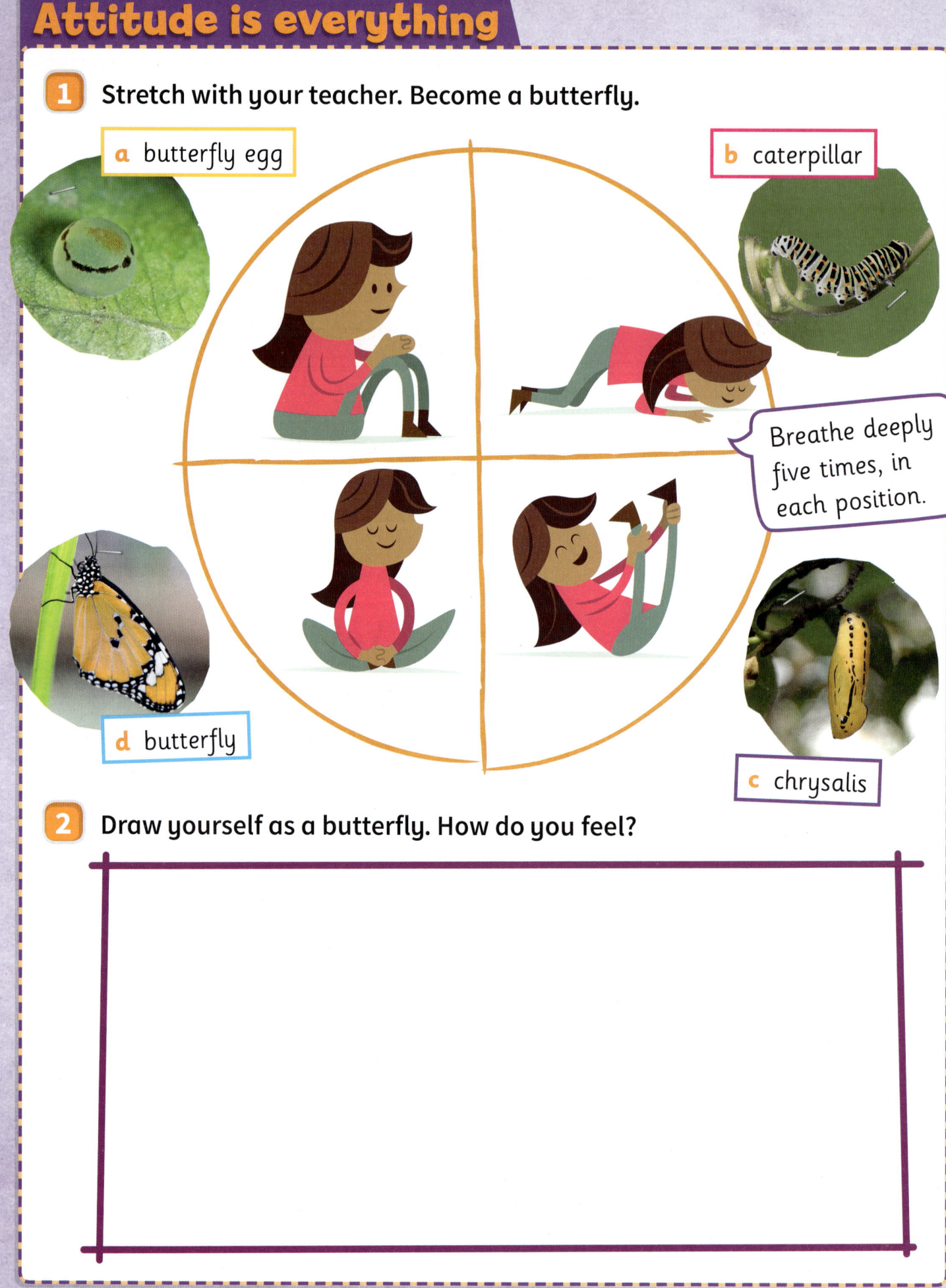

Now I know

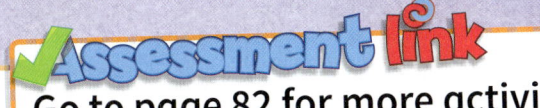

Go to page 82 for more activities.

1 Look and read. Choose the correct words and write them on the lines.

mammals

amphibians

molluscs

carnivores

a These animals have got fur or hair. _____
b These animals haven't got a backbone. _____
c These animals eat meat. _____
d These animals lay eggs in water. _____

2 🎧 Listen and number. Write the name.

_____   _____

Chant
Arthropod band

I am Jane Goodall.
I study chimpanzees in their natural habitat.

ARE ALL PLANTS THE SAME?

Match the photos to the correct words.

They are tall. They have got thick **trunks**, branches and leaves.

Farmers grow some plants.

They are short and have lots of **stems**.

We can eat some plants.

It is green and bendy.

Some plants grow everywhere.

- grass
- trees
- edible
- bushes
- cultivated
- wild

Mini-project

Try it out

Let's make a plant mural.

1 Bring plants or photos of plants to school.

2 Work in groups and create a mural.

What have I learnt?

We classify plants in different ways:
A _____ and _____ are types of plants.
Plants can be _____ or _____ .
We can eat _____ plants.

MY DICTIONARY

bush

cultivated

edible

grass

wild

HAS IT GOT LEAVES?

Trace the words.

Some trees lose their leaves in autumn and winter. They are **deciduous**.

evergreen

deciduous

spring and summer

Some trees have got green leaves all year round. They are **evergreen**.

deciduous

evergreen

autumn and winter

Why do some trees lose their leaves in autumn?

FUN FACT

I am evergreen.

Me too!

Mini-project

Make your own deciduous tree!

1 Cut out the four trees from your worksheets.

2 Decorate one tree for each season and glue them together.

MY DICTIONARY

autumn

winter

deciduous

evergreen

What have I learnt?

_____ trees lose their leaves in _____ and _____ .
_____ trees do not lose their leaves.

WHERE ARE THE SEEDS?

Look at this flowering plant. Circle all the seeds.

Plants produce **seeds** inside the flower. The flower turns into a **fruit**, with the seeds inside.

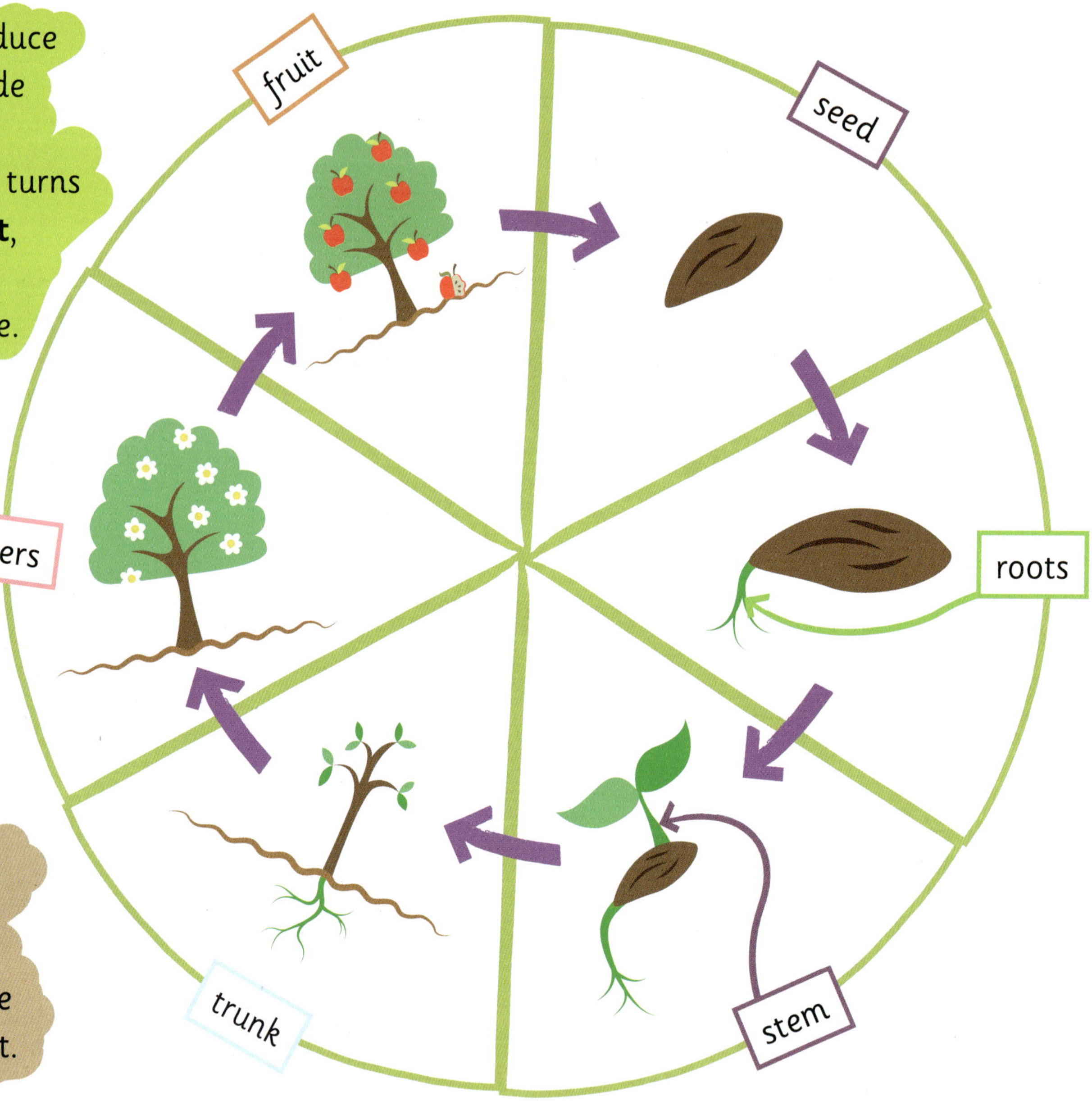

fruit

seed

flowers

roots

stem

trunk

Seeds on the ground can grow and become a new plant.

Where do plants keep their seeds?

Find the fungus hidden in the unit!

FUN FACT
There are big and small seeds.

I am your big brother!

Mini-project

Let's make a flap poster for the life cycle of a seed.

1 Cut and fold the paper. Write the numbers one to six on the flaps.

2 Draw and colour a stage inside each flap. Stick the flaps to coloured card.

Show it to your friends.

What have I learnt?

Some plants have got _____ .
Some of the flowers grow _____ to protect the seeds. Seeds in the ground grow _____ and a _____ .

MY DICTIONARY

flowers

fruit

roots

seeds

stem

WHAT ARE THE SPORES FOR?

Draw spores on the fern.

Some plants don't produce flowers or seeds. They are called **non-flowering** plants. Some non-flowering plants use **spores** to reproduce.

moss

How are flowering and non-flowering plants different?

ferns

spores

FUN FACT
Fungi use spores to reproduce, too!

Is it raining?

No! I am sporing.

Mini-project

Investigate and make a class fern.

1 Investigate ferns. Answer the questions.

   a Where are the spores on a fern leaf? _____
   b What colour are the spores? _____

2 Make a class fern.

   Cut out fern leaves from green card. Put brown plasticine spores on them.

Stick straws to your leaves.

Put the class' leaves together.

MY DICTIONARY

non-flowering

ferns

moss

spores

What have I learnt?

_____-_____ plants don't produce flowers or seeds. Some non-flowering plants use _____ to reproduce. _____ and _____ are non-flowering plants.

Attitude is everything

1 Sunflowers have very deep roots. They get everything they need from the soil, the sun and water. How do you get what you need? Draw.

2 Colour the mandala.

How are you feeling today?

_____

How are you feeling now?

Now I know

Go to page 84 for more activities.

1 Circle the correct option.

| wild   cultivated | grass   bush | edible   inedible |

2 🎧 Listen and tick (✓).

1 What type of plant is it?

2 What plant did Joe bring to school?

Chant
Mosses and roses

I am Beatrix Potter.
I loved writing stories and collecting plants. I had a great garden!

WHERE DOES IT COME FROM?

Find out

Trace the materials that are made from plants.

Natural materials

Natural materials come from **nature**: animals, plants and rocks.

- wool
- cotton
- wood
- petroleum
- rock
- sand

Manufactured materials

People make natural materials into **manufactured** (non-natural) materials.

- fabric
- paper
- plastic
- metal
- glass

Project Step 1

Make a materials display.

1 Bring objects to class in clear plastic bags.

2 Classify your objects. Tell your class where you found them.

I found this rock in the park. It is a natural material.

What have I learnt?

We use natural materials to make manufactured materials.
Some natural materials are wool, cotton and wood.
Some manufactured materials are _____, _____, _____, _____ and _____.

MY DICTIONARY

fabric

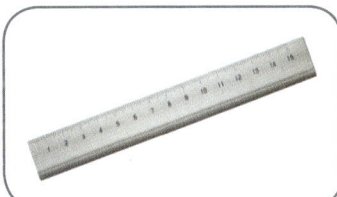
glass

metal

paper

plastic

WHAT ARE THEY GOOD FOR?

Circle the opposite of *rigid*.

Materials have got different **properties**. We choose the best material for each object.

Find out

- soft
- hard
- flexible
- rigid
- transparent
- opaque

Find the hard hat hidden in the unit!

FUN FACT

Umbrellas need to be waterproof!

Project Step 2

Label your object.

1 Observe your object. Write its name and properties.

2 Label your bag and stick it to the poster.

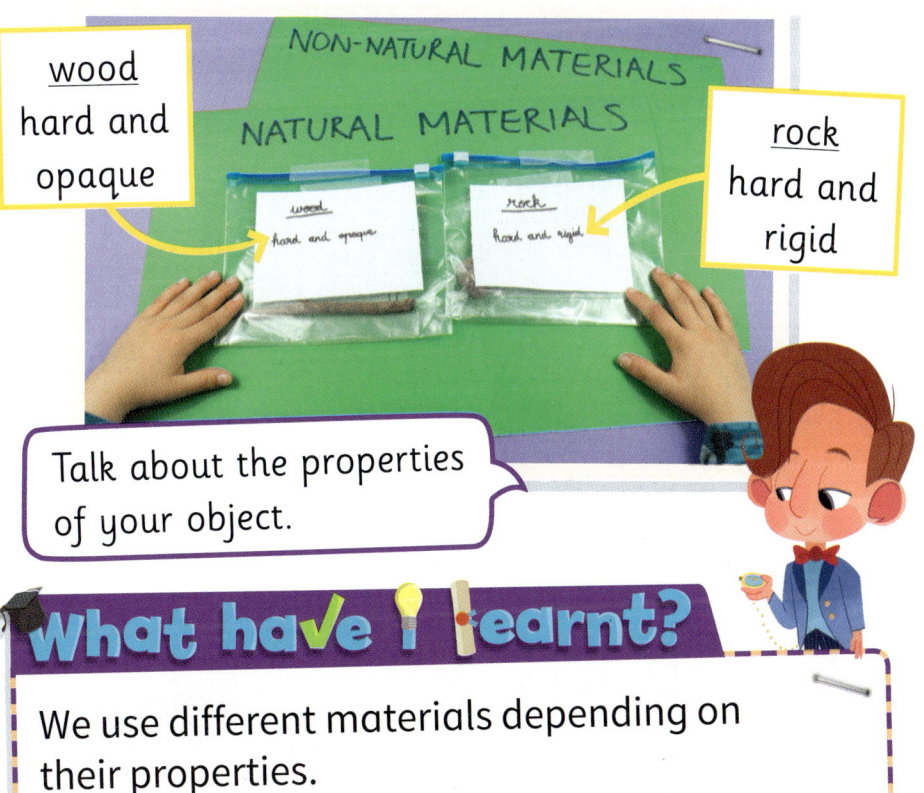

wood hard and opaque

rock hard and rigid

Talk about the properties of your object.

What have I learnt?

We use different materials depending on their properties.
Materials can be _____, _____, _____, _____ or _____.

MY DICTIONARY

flexible

hard

rigid

soft

transparent

WHAT IS YOUR HOME MADE OF?

Find out

🎧 Listen. What is each home made of? Match.

We use different **materials** to build homes in different parts of the world.

ice

In the forest, some people live in huts.

In the desert, some people live in tents.

Why are these homes made of these materials?

concrete

wood

fabric

In towns and villages, some people live in houses or flats.

In the Arctic, some people live in igloos.

Do you know other types of homes?

FUN FACT
The oldest house in England is made of stone.

60

Mini-project

Build a house.

1 Choose and write the materials for your house.

2 Colour your house and cut it out.

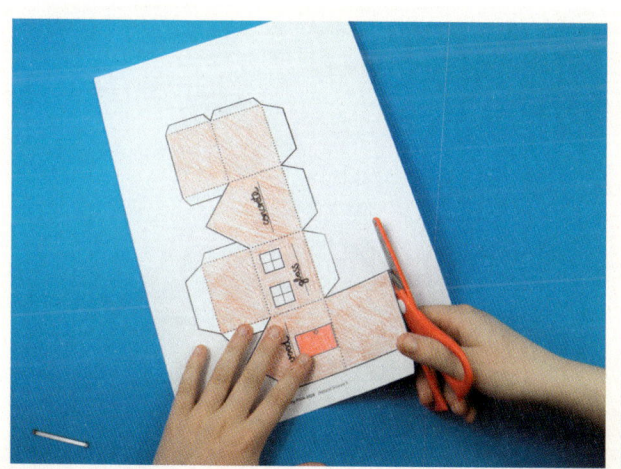

MY DICTIONARY

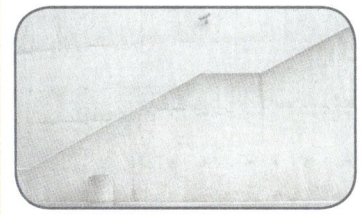
concrete

flats

huts

igloos

tents

What have I learnt?

Around the world, there are different types of homes. In the forest, there are _____ .
In the Arctic, there are _____ .
In the desert, there are _____ and we live in houses or _____ made of _____ .

HOW DO MATERIALS CHANGE?

Find out

Colour the reversible changes blue and the irreversible changes green.

We can change the form of materials. There are **reversible** and **irreversible** changes.

How can we change materials?

reversible
With reversible changes, materials can return to the same form.

heat · liquid · solid · cool

irreversible
With irreversible changes, materials cannot return to the same form.

soft · heat · hard · cool

heat and cool

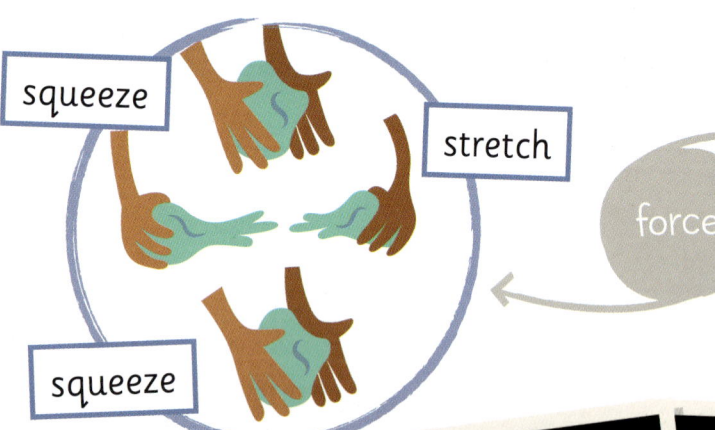

squeeze · stretch · squeeze

force

"We will never be the same."

FUN FACT
Eggs are irreversible.

Let's learn more about reversible and irreversible changes.

1

heat it → liquid → cool it

What happens? Draw.

Is it a reversible or irreversible change? It is _____ .

2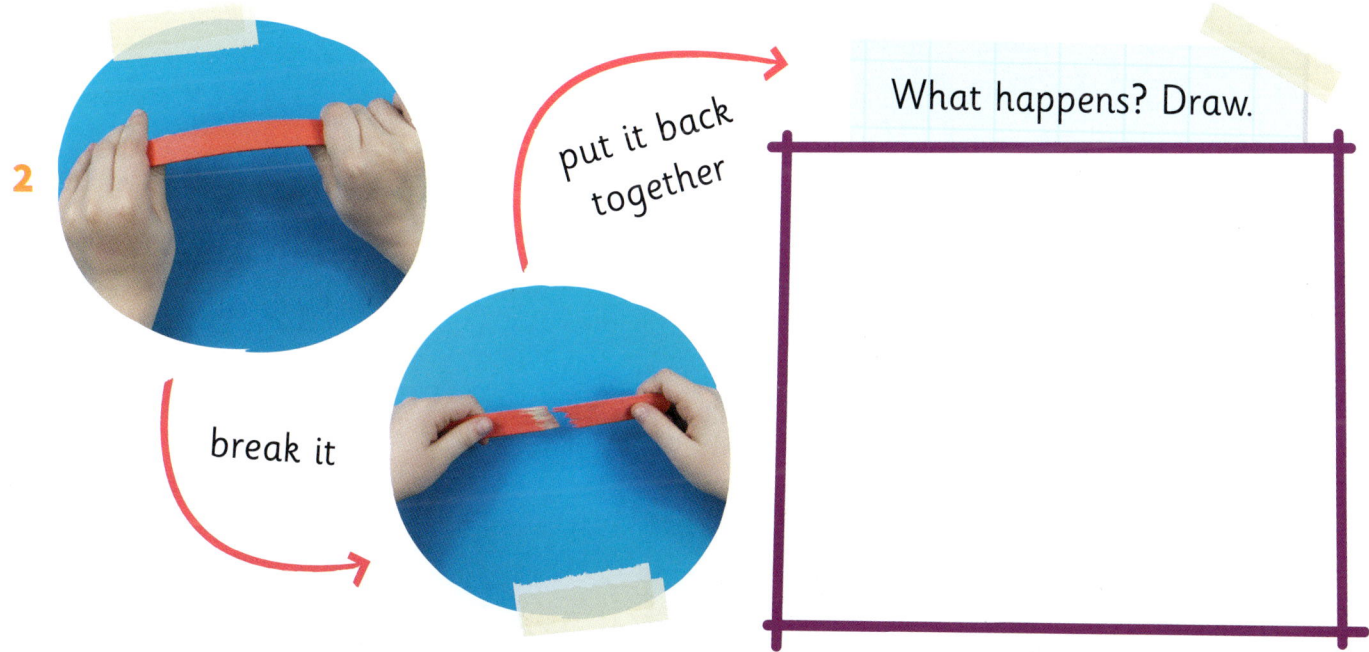

break it → put it back together

What happens? Draw.

Is it a reversible or irreversible change? It is _____ .

Attitude is everything

1 **Let's make a flower vase.**

1 Find a plastic bottle. Decorate it.

2 Colour and decorate cupcake papers.

3 Stick plastic straws to the centre of the cupcake papers.

Reduce Reuse Recycle

Now you can take your flowers home!

Now I know

Assessment link
Go to page 86 for more activities.

1 Tick (✓) the correct properties.

Materials				
soft				
hard				
flexible				
rigid				
transparent				
opaque				

2 🎧 Listen and tick (✓) the box.

1 What is the cup made of?

2 How is Mark protected from the rain?

Chant
Irreversible

I am Gustave Eiffel.
I was an engineer. I built the Eiffel Tower in Paris.

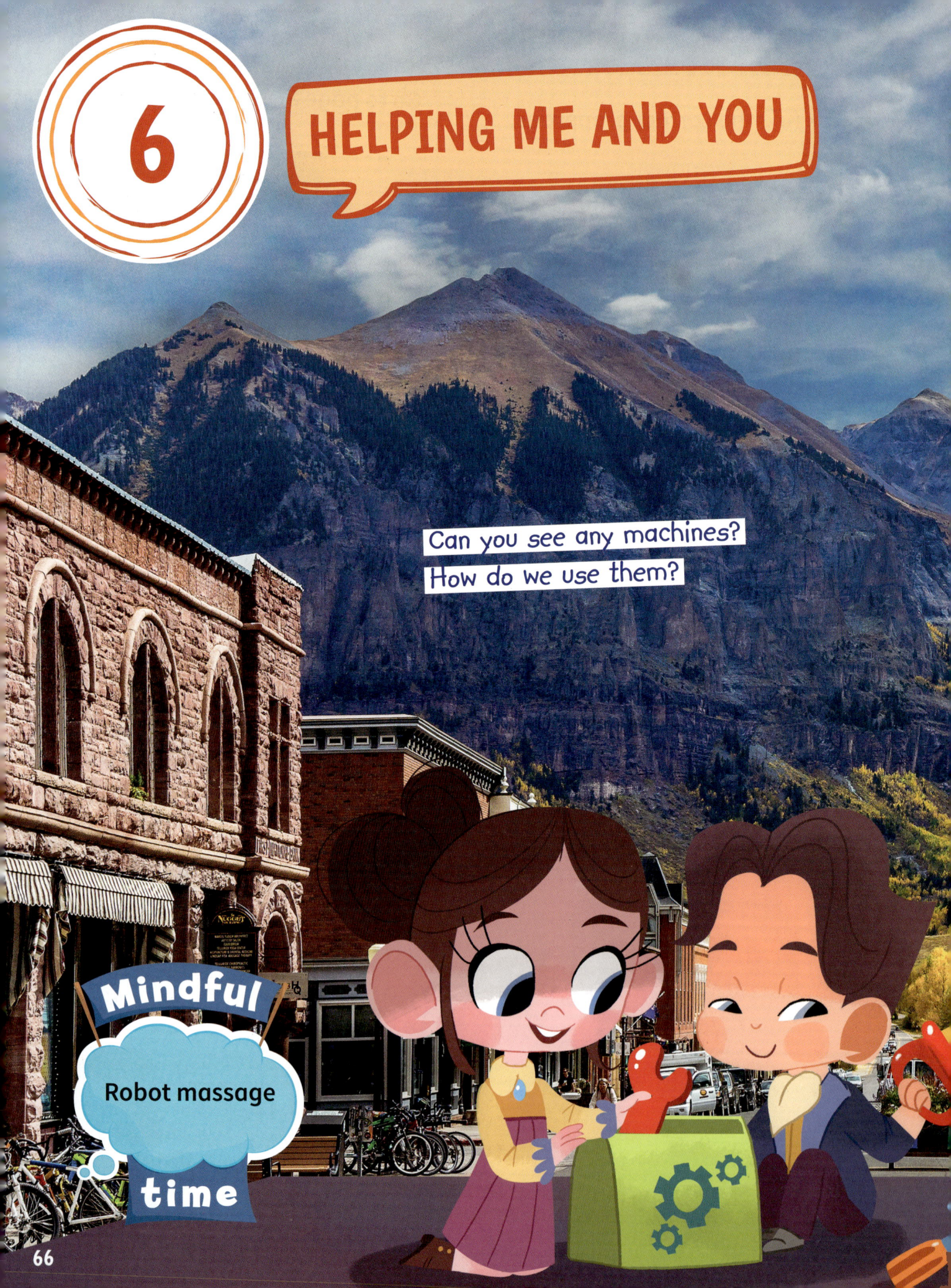

CAN YOU FIX A TAP?

Find out

Circle the tools you use at home.

Some **tools** are simple. They have only got one or two parts. They work using our **energy**. We can pull, turn, push or twist them. Tools help us every day.

Which tools do we need to be careful with?

- hammer
- spanner
- saw
- screwdriver
- pencil
- Kitchen

Which tools can we use to fix the tap?

Find the hammer hidden in the unit!

FUN FACT

Hey! I am a tool, too!

68

Mini-project

Let's make a tool mini book.

1 Prepare your mini book. Think about the tools you want to include.

2 Draw a tool on each page. Write its name.

MY DICTIONARY

hammer

saw

screwdriver

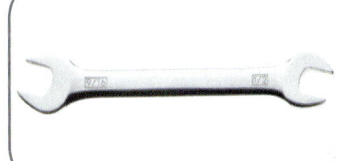
spanner

What have I learnt?

Tools are simple objects with one or two parts. We can fix things with a _____ , _____ , _____ or _____ . They make our lives easier.

69

HOW ARE THEY DIFFERENT?

🎧 Listen and circle the complex machines.

Machines have got different parts. The different parts work together, like a team, to do a job.

crane

inclined plane

There are **simple** and **complex** machines. Simple machines have got few or no moving parts. They work with human energy.

Complex machines have got lots of parts. They need **mains electricity** or **batteries** to work. Machines make our lives easier.

escalator

pulley

Is an aeroplane a complex or a simple machine?

I'm burnt.

FUN FACT
Before toasters, people toasted bread over a fire.

> Let's have a race!

1 Which inclined plane do you think is faster? Discuss with your partner.

2 Test the inclined planes with a toy car. Were you correct?

> Which inclined plane do you think is easier to climb?

DO YOU HAVE THE ENERGY?

Find out

Circle the machines that use batteries.

We use machines every day. **Complex** machines use different types of energy.

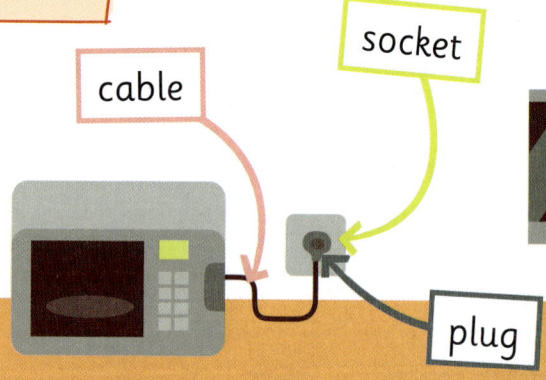

switch • cable • socket • plug • batteries

Some machines use mains electricity.

What other machines do you use?

Some machines use batteries.

What types of energy do they use?

Some machines use human energy.

Game Zone

Let's play a matching game.

1 Make cards for machines and cards for the type of energy they use.

2 Colour the pictures and play the game with your partner.

MY DICTIONARY

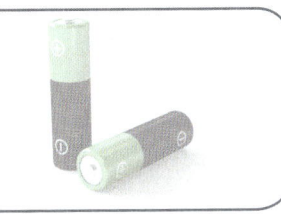
batteries

mains electricity

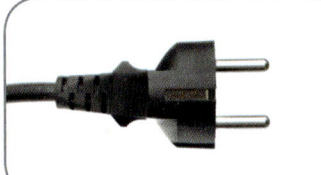
plug

socket

switch

What have I learnt?

Complex machines need _____ _____ or _____ to work. Some complex machines have a cable and a _____ . We plug them into a _____ . Sometimes, we use a _____ to turn them on.

HOW DO THEY CHANGE OUR WORLD?

What does this invention look like now? Draw.

Inventions get better over time. They change our lives and the world!

FIRE

PAST ● ——————————————————— ● PRESENT

THE WHEEL

PAST ● ——————————————————— ● PRESENT

THE PLOUGH

Which is the best invention?

Do you use these inventions?

Mini-project

Try it out

Let's invent!

1 Build a robot with recycled materials.

2 Compare your robot and the robot in the photo. Tick (✓).

	My robot	The other robot
has one or two parts		
has lots of parts		
uses a battery		
uses mains electricity		
uses human energy		

Is your robot a simple or a complex machine?

MY DICTIONARY

fire

wheel

plough

telephone

past

present

What have I learnt?

F_____, the _____ and the _____ are inventions from the _____ , but they are different in the _____ .

Attitude is everything

1 Draw a smiley face (☺) or a sad face (☹). Put a red cross (✗) through the dangerous actions.

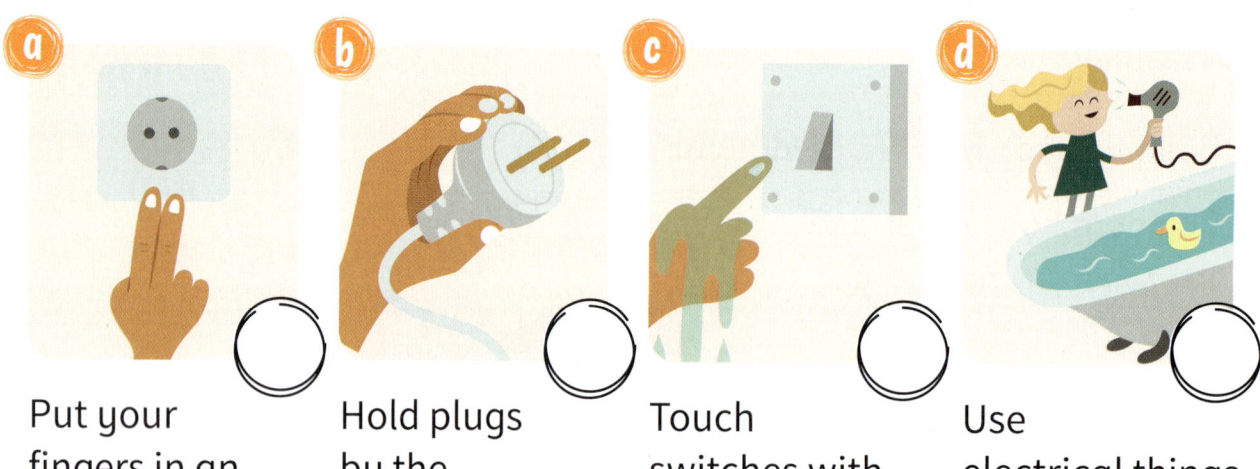

a. Put your fingers in an electric socket.

b. Hold plugs by the plastic part.

c. Touch switches with wet hands.

d. Use electrical things near water.

2 How can you save electricity? Tick (✓).

Now I know

Assessment link
Go to page 88 for more activities.

1 🎧 Listen and number.

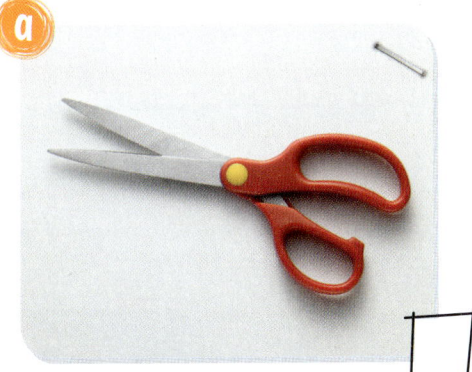
a

b

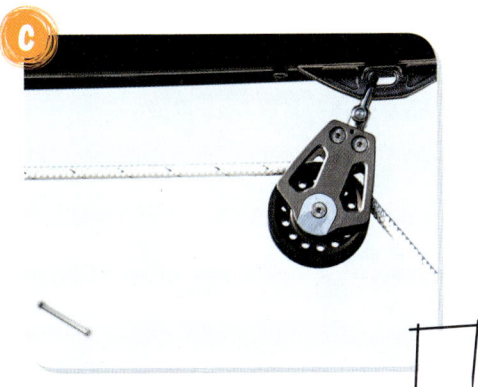
c

d

2 Look and read and write.

a There are some tools in the _____ .

b There is a complex machine on the _____ floor.

c John is opening a can. He is using a _____ machine.

Chant
Energy

I am Amelia Earhart.
I was a pilot. I was the first woman to fly alone across the Atlantic Ocean.

1 Let's review

Find the right words

1 Match.

1 Wear a helmet when you ride your bike.

2 Wear a hat when you are in the sun.

3 Wear knee pads when you play football.

2 Find the words.

| muscle | joint | bone | limb | skull | torso |

m	q	y	r	w	g	u	o	b	m	t
u	l	y	t	j	a	q	b	o	g	o
s	k	h	w	t	o	l	u	n	f	r
c	j	j	s	h	z	i	y	e	s	s
l	i	m	b	l	j	y	n	p	a	o
e	g	z	s	d	f	g	h	t	q	b
t	f	s	k	u	l	l	t	r	z	h

Look back

1 🎧 Listen and colour and write.

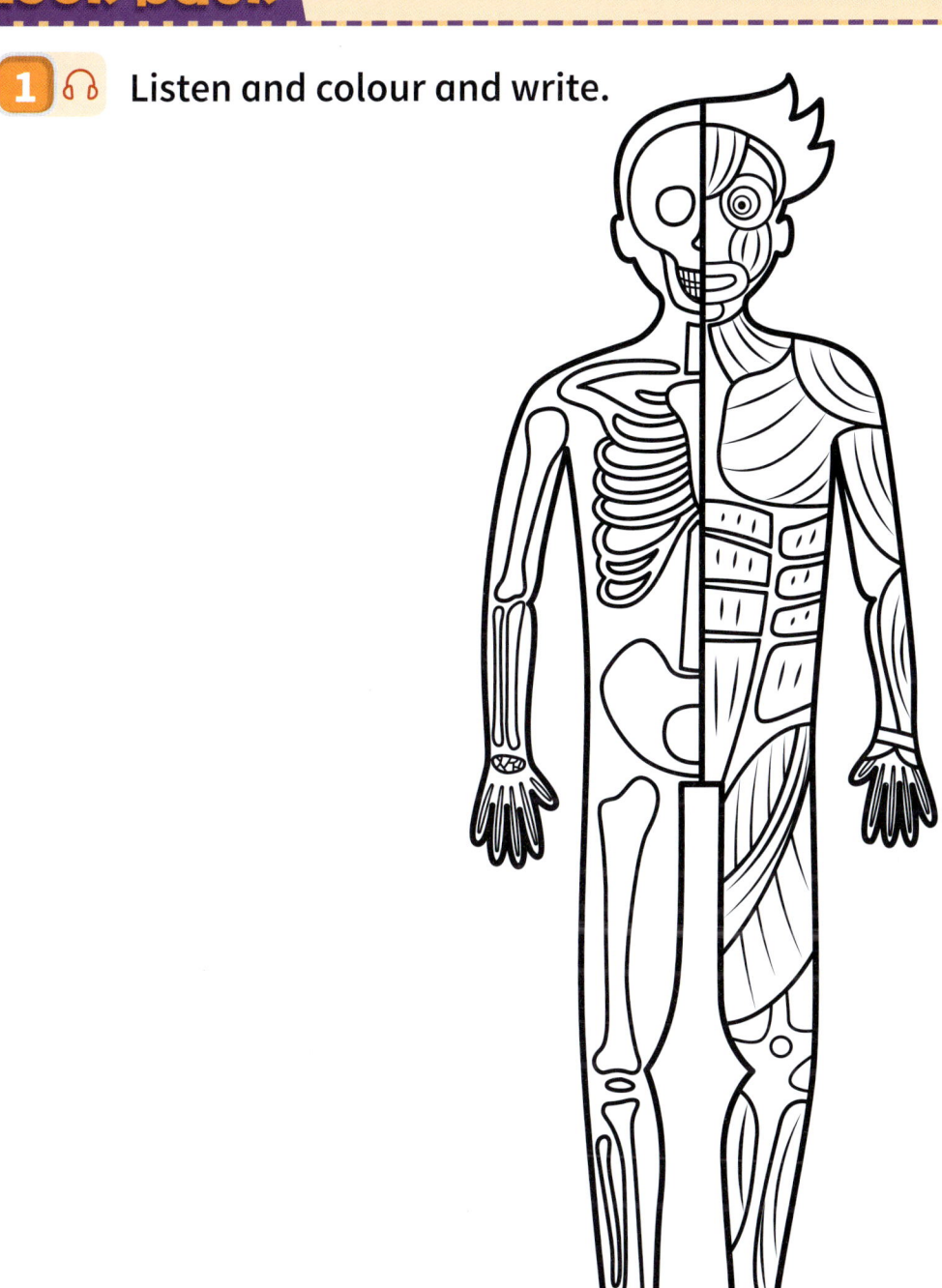

2 Correct the words in bold.

a Your mouth is in your **torso**. _____

b A pectoral is a **bone**. _____

c The skull is a **joint**. _____

d Your jaw is a **muscle**. _____

e Legs are your **upper** limbs. _____

2 Let's review

Find the right words

1 🎧 Read, listen and complete. Use the words in the box.

sweet   salty   bitter

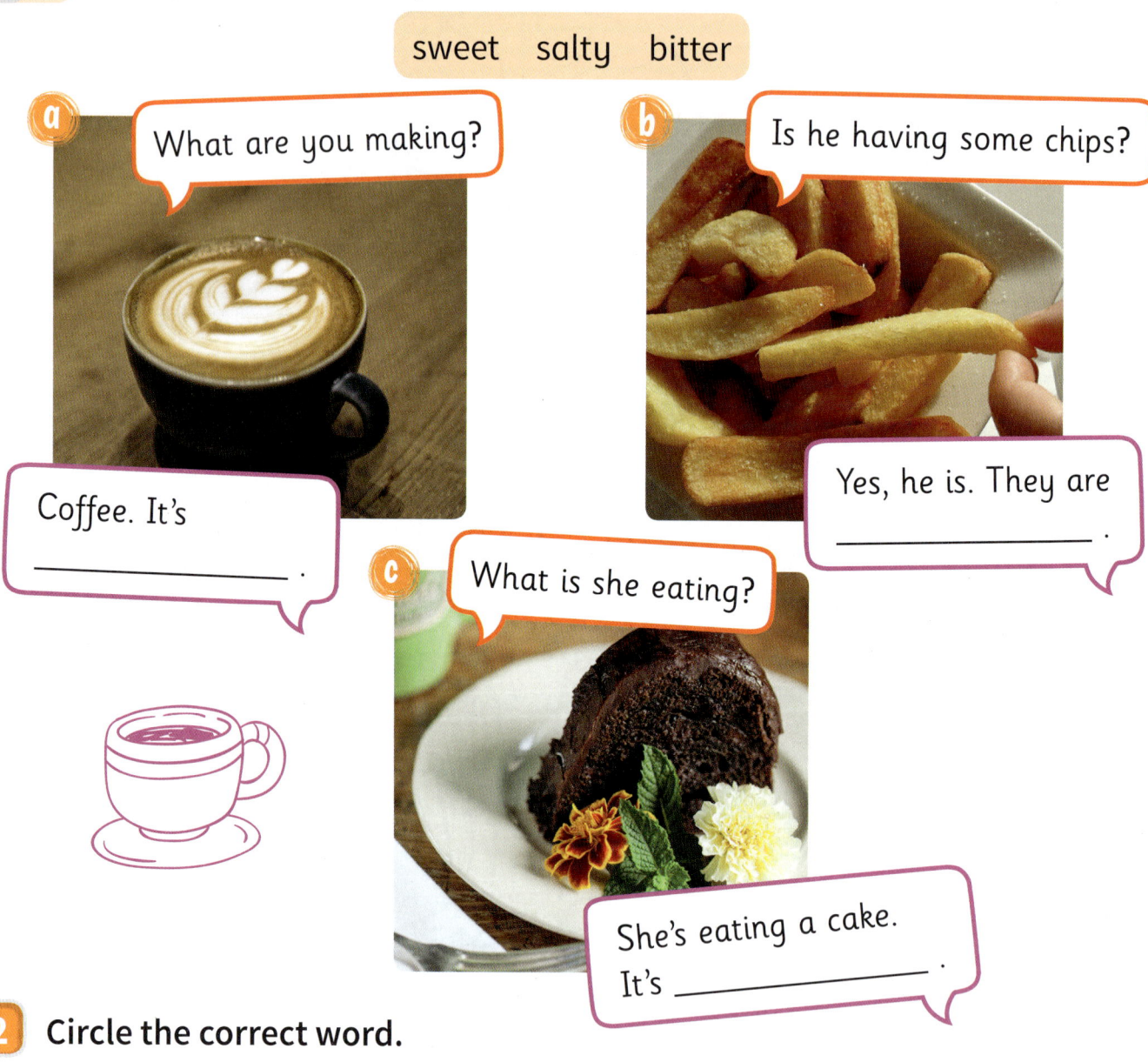

a What are you making?
Coffee. It's _____.

b Is he having some chips?
Yes, he is. They are _____.

c What is she eating?
She's eating a cake. It's _____.

2 Circle the correct word.
a He can *see* / *sees* colours.
b The small intestine *absorb* / *absorbs* nutrients.
c We *breathe* / *breathes* air.
d The heart *pump* / *pumps* blood around the body.
e When babies *is* / *are* born, they drink milk.

Look back

1 Look and read. Choose the correct words and write them on the lines.

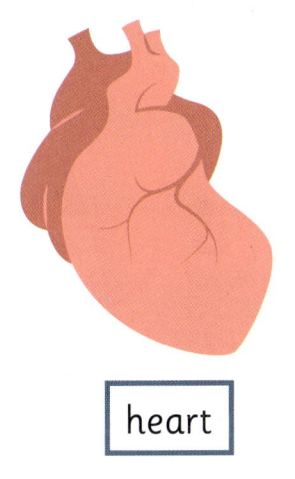

heart

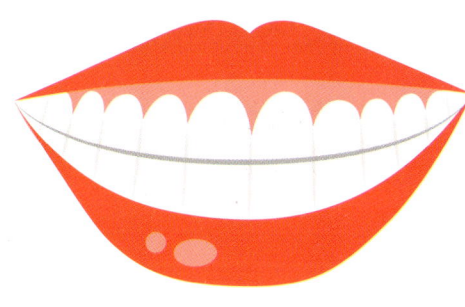

teeth

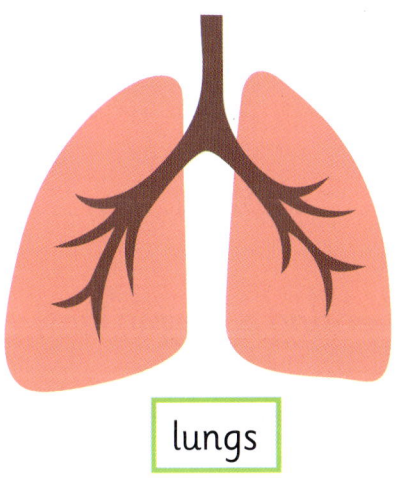

lungs

large intestine

a We use these to chew food. _____
b This part of the stomach transports waste. _____
c Air travels to these organs. _____
d This organ pumps blood around the body. _____

2 Write *yes* or *no*.

I can taste with my ears. _____

I can smell with my nose. _____

I can hear with my hands. _____

I can see with my eyes. _____

I can touch with my hands. _____

3 Let's review

Find the right words

1 🎧 Listen and circle the correct option.

a There *is / is being* a frog in the pond.
b The frog *jumps / is jumping* from one rock to another.
c Some bees *fly / are flying* in the sky.
d Look! There *is / is being* a snail! It *eats / is eating* a purple leaf!
e A boy *looks / is looking* at it.

2 Complete using *Why* and *Because*.

a _____ have amphibians got gills?
_____ they use gills to breathe in water.

b _____ do sharks swim?
_____ they are fish and they live in water.

c _____ do worms slither?
_____ they haven't got any legs.

Look back

1 Look and read. Choose the correct words and write them on the lines.

a snake

a zebra

a crab

a It has got an exoskeleton and ten legs.
_____

b It is a reptile. You can see it in the jungle.
_____

c It is a mammal. It has got black and white stripes.
_____

2 Complete the sentences. Use the words in the box.

> fish   amphibians   molluscs   birds   mammals   arthropods

a Some animals, like _____ , are born live.
b Other animals, like fish, arthropods, molluscs, reptiles and _____ , are born from eggs.
c Reptiles and _____ have scales.
d _____ live in water and on land. They have got wet skin and breathe with lungs and gills.
e Many _____ have got antennae.
f Arthropods and _____ haven't got bones. They are invertebrates.

4 Let's review

Find the right words

1 🎧 **Listen, read and complete the season.**

a It's windy. Deciduous trees are losing their leaves.
   It's _____ .

b It's hot. Deciduous and evergreen trees have got all their leaves.
   It's _____ .

c It's cold. Evergreen trees keep their leaves.
   It's _____ .

d It's warm. Deciduous trees are growing new leaves.
   It's _____ .

2 **Look at the pictures and complete the sentences. Use the words in the box.**

sometimes   always   never   often

a Evergreen plants _____ lose their leaves.

b _____ plants don't produce flowers or seeds.

c Deciduous plants _____ lose their leaves in autumn and winter.

d Farmers _____ grow edible plants.

Look back

1 Look and read and write.

a What is the dog eating?
_____ .

b How many bushes are there?
_____ .

c What can you see in the basket? _____ .

d The man is planting some
_____ .

Now write a sentence about the picture.

_____
_____
_____ .

2 Look, read and circle.

a It's a *bush* / *tree*.

b It's *cultivated* / *wild*.

c It's *edible* / *inedible*.

d It's a *flowering* / *non-flowering* plant.

5 Let's review

Find the right words

1 Look at the photos and complete the sentences. Use the words in the box.

> harder   rigid   softer   flexible

a A pillow is _____ than a metal tube.

b Plastic is more _____ than wood.

c Metal is more _____ than paper.

d Wood is _____ than a pillow.

2 Circle the correct option.

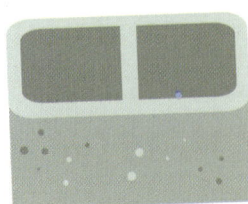

a Concrete is *rigid / flexible*.

b An igloo is made of *concrete / ice*.

c Wood is *hard / soft*.

Look back

1 🎧 Listen and colour and write.

2 Match.

a soft

b rigid

c transparent

d flexible

87

6 Let's review

Find the right words

1 Circle the correct option.

a You *must* / *mustn't* put your fingers in a socket.

b You *have to* / *don't have to* use a saw to cut wood.

c You *have to* / *don't have to* wear suncream on a cloudy day.

d You *must* / *mustn't* use a hairdryer to dry your face.

e You *must* / *mustn't* be careful when plugging something into a socket.

2 🎧 Listen and tick (✓) the box.

1 What is the spoon made of?

2 Who do the scissors belong to?

3 Which tool does Helen need?

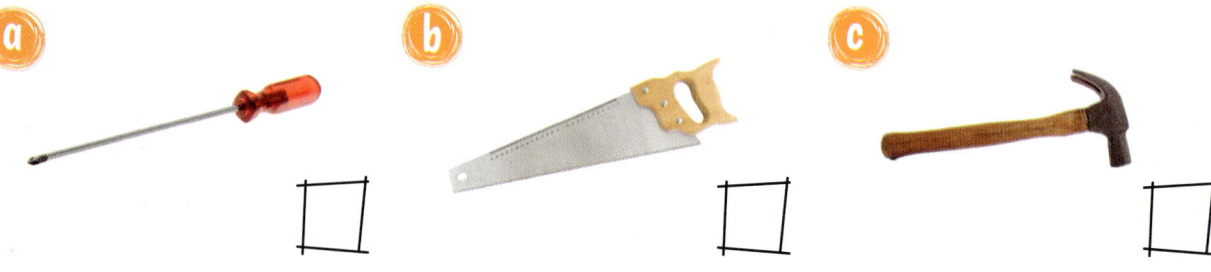

Look back

1 Read the text. Choose the right words and write them on the lines.

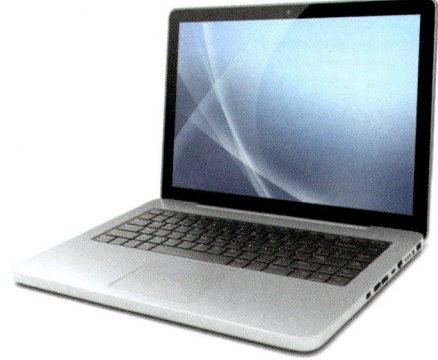

Computers are **(a)** _____ machines. They have **(b)** _____ of parts. They use **(c)** _____ . They are made of metal, glass and **(d)** _____ . They are a great **(e)** _____ !

a	complete	complex	simple
b	one	few	lots
c	food	human energy	electricity
d	plastic	wood	paper
e	invent	invention	invented

2 Draw machines that use …

[human energy]

[batteries]

[mains electricity]

Story 1

🎧 **Listen and read.**

Little Braille and Little da Vinci are at the gym.
I will be a great athlete.
I will be your trainer.

Let's go to the sports field!

Two hours later …
My body aches.
That's a good sign!

My heart is strong.
I can't say the same!

Your lungs are full of oxygen.

I'm going to take part in the Olympic Games.
Find a new trainer!

Now act out the story!

Now I know

1 Order the story. Write numbers in the boxes.

2 Which organs are they taking care of? Tick (✓) the boxes.

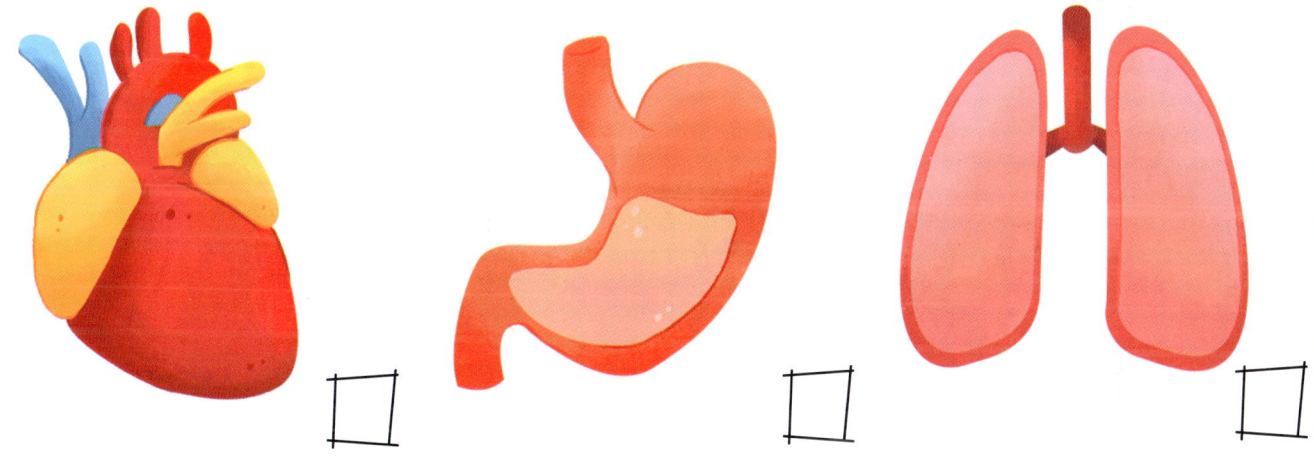

3 Do you like the story? Colour the medals.

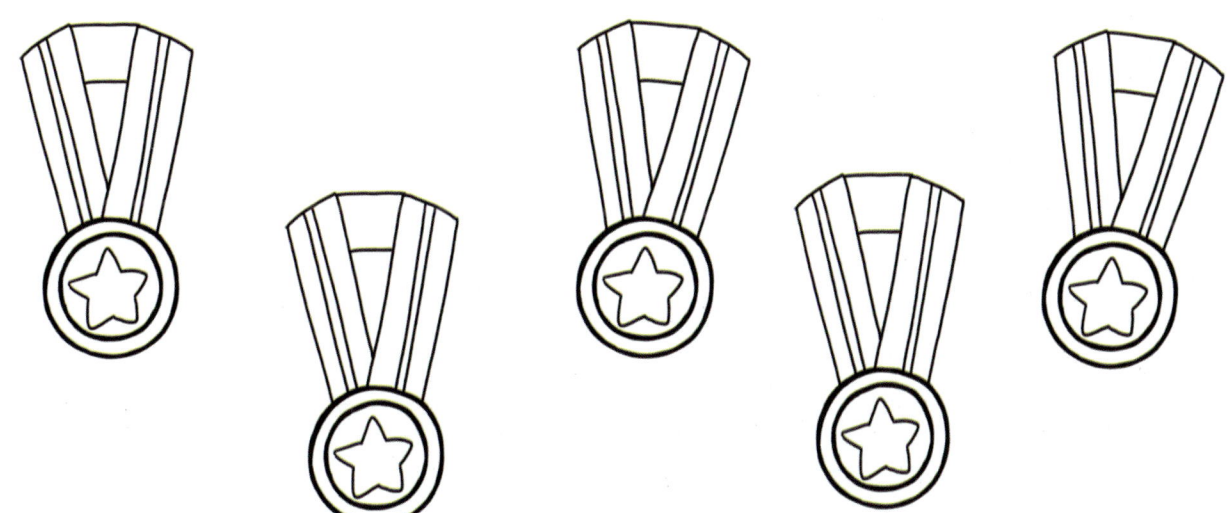

Story 2

🎧 Listen and read.

Now act out the story!

Now I know

1 Order the story. Write numbers in the boxes.

2 Which two non-flowering plants can you see in the story? Tick (✓) the boxes.

3 Do you like the story? Colour the chimpanzees.

Story 3

🎧 **Listen and read.**

Now act out the story!

Now I know

1 Order the story. Write numbers in the boxes.

2 Draw the materials and tools that Little Eiffel could use to build the cage.

Tools

Materials

3 Do you like the story? Colour the tools.

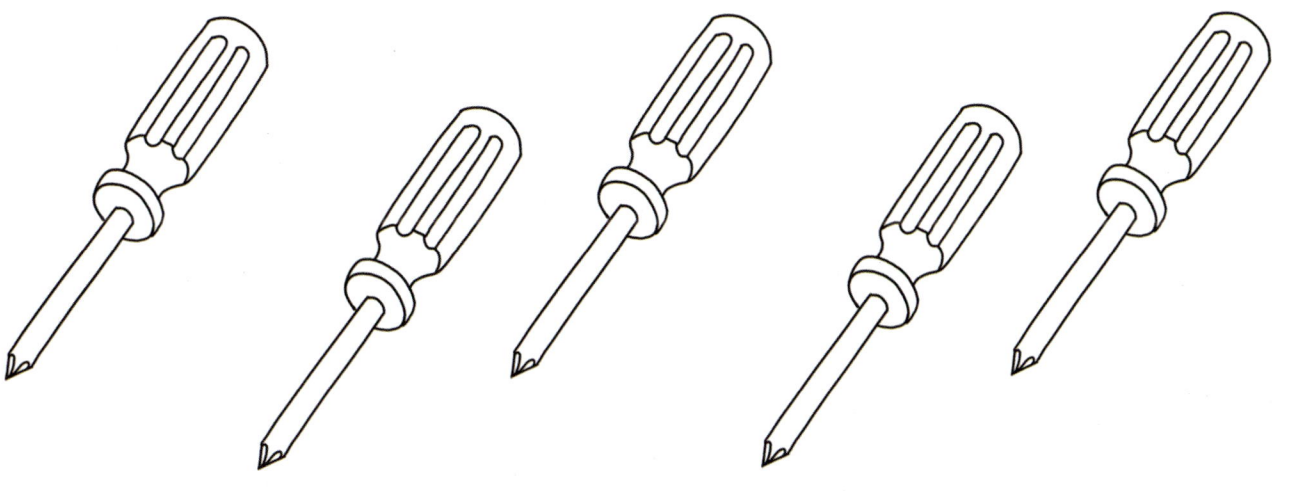

CAMBRIDGE UNIVERSITY PRESS

Acknowledgements

The authors and publishers acknowledge the following sources of copyright material and are grateful for the permissions granted. While every effort has been made, it has not always been possible to identify the sources of all the material used, or to trace all copyright holders. If any omissions are brought to our notice, we will be happy to include the appropriate acknowledgements on reprinting and in the next update to the digital edition, as applicable.

Photo acknowledgements

All images are sourced from Getty Images.

p. 2: Dukas/Universal Images Group; p. 2, p. 33: GK Hart/Vikki Hart/DigitalVision; p. 3, pp. 42–43: paul mansfield photography/Moment; p. 5: Stockbyte, carlacdesign/iStock/Getty Images Plus, ONYXprj/iStock/Getty Images Plus, MarinaMariya/iStock/Getty Images Plus, lolya88/iStock/Getty Images Plus, muuraa/iStock/Getty Images Plus, Handini_Atmodiwiryo/iStock/Getty Images Plus, Nahhan/iStock/Getty Images Plus; p. 5, p. 8, p. 10, p. 11, p. 21: ourlifelooklikeballoon/iStock/Getty Images Plus; p. 5, p. 25, p. 38, p. 58, p. 80: LokFung/DigitalVision Vectors; p. 5, p. 13: Zdenek Sasek/iStock/Getty Images Plus; p. 8: jesadaphorn/iStock/Getty Images Plus; kowalska-art/iStock/Getty Images Plus, Tom Merton/OJO Images; p. 9: Ronnie Kaufman/Larry Hirshowitz/Blend Images, Jamie Grill, Pando HallPhotographer's Choice; p. 9, p. 17, p. 32, p. 38, p. 41, p. 46, p. 56, p. 65, p. 76, p. 83: Westend61; p. 10, p. 23, p. 69, p. 89: lineartestpilot/iStock/Getty Images Plus; p. 12: Rubberball/Mike Kemp; p. 14: Olly-Molly/iStock/Getty Images Plus, Rubberball/Erik Isakson; p. 15: GennadiiKorchuganov/iStock/Getty Images Plus; p. 16: csakisti/iStock/Getty Images Plus, saz1977/iStock/Getty Images Plus, joebelanger/iStock/Getty Images Plus; p. 17: Culture Club/Hulton Archive; pp. 18–19: kevinjeon00/E+; p. 20: Gal_Istvan/iStock/Getty Images Plus, Obaba/iStock/Getty Images Plus, Nataleana/iStock/Getty Images Plus; p. 21: Sebalos/iStock/Getty Images Plus, Huw Jones/Photolibrary, Evgeniy Skripnichenko/iStock/Getty Images PlusHuw Jones/Photolibrary, samsonovs/iStock/Getty Images Plus; p. 22: kolesnikovserg/iStock/Getty Images Plus, StockPhotosArt/iStock/Getty Images Plus, pashapixel/iStock/Getty Images Plus, audumbla/iStock/Getty Images Plus; p. 23: SEBASTIAN KAULITZKI/SCIENCE PHOTO LIBRARY, SPRINGER MEDIZIN/SCIENCE PHOTO LIBRARY, decade3d/iStock/Getty Images Plus, janulla/iStock/Getty Images Plus, yodiyim/iStock/Getty Images Plus; p. 24: Nataleanac/iStock/Getty Images Plus; p. 25: Andrew Brookes/Cultura, jack0m/DigitalVision Vectors, adjichanda471/iStock/Getty Images Plus, lukaves/iStock/Getty Images Plus, p. 26: Kudryashka/iStock/Getty Images Plus, LWA/Larry Williams/Blend Images, Wavebreakmedia/iStock/Getty Images Plus, Marvin Fox/Moment, Granger Wootz/Blend Images, Juanmonino/E+, Science Photo Library; p. 27: FamVeld/iStock/Getty Images Plus, Yobro10/iStock/Getty Images Plus, Morsa Images/DigitalVision, Julien McRoberts/Blend Images; p. 27, p. 38: Topic Images Inc; p. 29, p. 71: FrankRamspott/DigitalVision Vectors; p. 29: Science Photo Library - PASIEKA/Brand X Pictures, PIXOLOGICSTUDIO/SCIENCE PHOTO LIBRARY, JW LTD/Taxi, elitzaguntcheva/RooM, Cultura RM Exclusive/Uwe Umstaetter, Photos.com/Getty Images Plus; p. 30: Ger Bosma/Moment; p. 31: Christopher Jimenez Nature Photo/Moment; p. 32: PHOTOSTOCK-ISRAEL/SCIENCE PHOTO LIBRARY, Nick Brundle Photography/Moment; p. 33: Sudowoodo/iStock/Getty Images Plus, Sasha Bell/Moment, 3drenderings/iStock/Getty Images Plus, Mario Gutiérrez/Moment; p. 34: Premium/Universal Images Group, wrangel/iStock/Getty Images Plus; p. 35: DEA/S. VANNINI/De Agostini, Doug Meikle Dreaming Track Images/Oxford Scientific, wildestanimal/Moment, Tom Brakefield/Corbis Documentary, georgeclerk/iStock/Getty Images Plus; p. 36, p. 83: GlobalP/iStock/Getty Images Plus; p. 36: Jonathan Knowles/Stone, Digital Zoo/DigitalVision, American Images Inc/Stone, Robert Trevis-Smith/Moment; p. 36, p. 82: Simon Murrell/Cultura; p. 37: misterelements/iStock/Getty Images Plus, Jasius/Moment, Nil Raths/EyeEm, Lawrie Williams/Lonely Planet Images, LaDora Sims/Moment; p. 38: macy75/DigitalVision Vectors, Greg Pease/Photographer's Choice, Callista Images/Cultura, Kevin Summers/Photographer's Choice, Fernando Trabanco Fotografía/Moment, Neil Hewitt/EyeEm, moodboard/Cultura; p. 39: tanshy/iStock/Getty Images Plus, Anton Petrus/Moment, Luca Bertolacci/EyeEm; p. 40: Paul Starosta/Corbis Documentary, Tatiane Noviski Fornel/Moment, AlexTurton/Moment; p. 40, p. 75: Marka/Universal Images Group; p. 41: Steve Hoskins/The Image Bank, Mike Kemp, Andrew John Simpson/Stone, Craig Dingle/iStock/Getty Images Plus, Sylvain Gaboury/FilmMagic; p. 44: Little_Airplane/iStock/Getty Images Plus, Ian.CuiYi/Moment, kruwt/iStock/Getty Images Plus, igorr1/iStock/Getty Images Plus, Henry Arden/Cultura, mikroman6/Moment; p. 45: Sunshine_Art/iStock/Getty Images Plus, Don Johnston, prohor08/iStock/Getty Images Plus, Phongphan Saelee/EyeEm, wydynd/iStock/Getty Images Plus; p. 45, p. 56: Douglas Sacha/Moment; p. 46: Adam Burton/robertharding, negatina/Moment, Serg_Velusceac/iStock/Getty Images Plus, mammuth/E+, Patricia Hamilton/Moment, Johner Images - Fridh, Conny/Brand X Pictures, Elizabeth Fernandez/Moment; p. 47: Vect0r0vich/iStock/Getty Images Plus, Sandra Clegg/Moment, Danielle Donders/Moment, Olivia Bell Photography/Moment, Anthony James/EyeEm, Ilona Nagy/Moment; p. 49: Dan Kitwood/Getty Images News, Michael Möller/EyeEm, ThomasVogel/E+, Linus Strandholm/EyeEm; p. 49, p. 68: pbombaert/Moment; p. 50: Visuals Unlimited, Inc./Nigel Cattlin, Relax Images/Cultura, Claire Plumridge/Moment; p. 51: Frank Carter/Lonely Planet Images, Mint Images/Mint Images RF, Boris SV/Moment, Antoni Agelet/Biosphoto; p. 53: Roger Stowell/Photolibrary, Prairie Pictures/The Image Bank, Luis Diaz Devesa/Moment, Cristian Bortes/EyeEm, Artemis/The Image Bank, Christian Horz/EyeEm, DEA/C.DANI/De Agostini Picture Library, Sally Williams Photography/Photographer's Choice, hsvrs/E+, Express Newspapers/Hulton Archive; p. 54: Mlenny/E+; p. 56: lucentius/iStock/Getty Images Plus, Zoran Milich/The Image Bank, LoveTheWind/iStock/Getty Images Plus, David Malan/Photographer's Choice, Claudia Viegas Schröder/EyeEm, funky-data/E+, Massimiliano Alessandro/EyeEm, PhonlamaiPhoto/iStock/Getty Images Plus; p. 56, p. 58: phototropic/E+; p. 57: rhkamen/Moment, foto-ruhrgebiet/iStock/Getty Images Plus, t_kimura/iStock/Getty Images Plus, Chee Siong The/EyeEm, Jose Manuel Espinola Aguayo/EyeEm; p. 58: Ng Sok Lian/EyeEm, Machado Noa/LightRocket, Joe Raedle/Getty Images News, Tim Boyle/Bloomberg, David Crane/iStock/Getty Images Plus; p. 59: Steve Russell/Toronto Star, DmitriyKazitsyn/iStock/Getty Images Plus, Don Mason/Blend Images, John Kuczala/DigitalVision, piovesempre/iStock/Getty Images Plus; p. 60: azzzya/iStock/Getty Images Plus, pixinoo/iStock/Getty Images Plus, Michael Marquand/Lonely Planet Images, vik898/iStock/Getty Images Plus, Edmund Sumner/VIEW/Passage; p. 61: veekicl/iStock/Getty Images Plus, Barbara Fischer, Australia/Moment, Yukinori Hasumi/Moment, DEA/V. GIANNELLA/De Agostini, RitaJ/iStock/Getty Images Plus, Mint Images RF; p. 62: Bildagentur-online/Universal Images Group; p. 63: Richard Bord/Getty Images Entertainment; p. 63, p. 84: Roberto Machado Noa/LightRocket; p. 65: imaginima/E+, Mark Viker/The Image Bank, Kristian Buus/In Pictures, Coprid/iStock/Getty Images Plus, Jack Taylor/Getty Images News, pada smith/iStock/Getty Images Plus, Tara Walton/Toronto Star, Monika Halinowska/Moment, NoDerog/iStock/Getty Images Plus, De Agostini Picture Library; pp. 66–67: Deb Snelson/Moment; p. 68: Dorling Kindersley, Vitalina/iStock/Getty Images Plus, xxmmxx/E+; p. 68, p. 88: dlerick/E+; p. 69: resonance/iStock/Getty Images Plus, avlntn/iStock/Getty Images Plus, MichaelJay/iStock/Getty Images Plus, EHStock/iStock/Getty Images Plus; p. 70: Geography Photos/Education Images/Universal Images Group, Karl Spencer/iStock/Getty Images Plus, Nicholas Eveleigh/Photodisc, DEA/M. SANTINI/De Agostini; p. 72: IAN HOOTON/Science Photo Library, Gavin Roberts/T3 Magazine/Future, sonorian/E+; p. 73: Stefan Kiefer/imageBROKER, Pongasn68/iStock/Getty Images Plus, deepblue4you/E+, Daft_Lion_Studio/E+, Image Source; p. 74: DEA/A. DAGLI ORTI/De Agostini, lucadp/iStock/Getty Images Plus, Henrik5000/iStock/Getty Images Plus, Veremeev/iStock/Getty Images Plus; p. 75: Oliver Burston/Ikon Images, tbradford/E+, Andrew Aitchison/Pictures Ltd./Corbis News, aluxum/E+, Olly Curtis/T3 Magazine/Future; p. 76: Spaces Images/Blend Images, The Sydney Morning Herald/Fairfax Media; p. 76, p. 80: Education Images/Universal Images Group; p. 77: Amendolagine Barracchia/AGF/Universal Images Group, Ana Elorza Irigoyen/Moment Mobile, gaspr13/E+, Neil Godwin/Future Publishing, Pictures Inc./The LIFE Picture Collection; p. 80: SOPA Images/LightRocket, Jeff Overs/BBC News & Current Affairs; p. 82: Prisma Bildagentur/Prisma by Dukas/Universal Images Group, bazilfoto/iStock/Getty Images Plus; p. 83: RODGER BOSCH/AFP, wildpixel/iStock/Getty Images Plus, LaDora Sims/Moment; p. 84: dmitry_7/iStock/Getty Images Plus, DEA/ARCHIVIO J. LANGE/De Agostini, DEA/D. DAGLI ORTI/De Agostini; p. 85: pkanchana/iStock/Getty Images Plus, vencavolrab/iStock/Getty Images Plus, Robin MacDougall, DEA/C. DANI/De Agostini; p. 87: ULTRA F/DigitalVision, Sebastian Kopp/EyeEm, artisteer/iStock/Getty Images Plus, Daniel Acker/Bloomberg; p. 88: Mohd Haniff Abas/EyeEm, slav/iStock/Getty Images Plus, damircudic/E+, Mel Yates/DigitalVision, Blend Images - KidStock/Brand X Pictures, deepblue4you/E+/iStock/Getty Images Plus, Iurii Garmash/iStock/Getty Images Plus, User2547783c_812/iStock/Getty Images Plus; p. 89: UmbertoPantalone/iStock/Getty Images Plus, Terriana/iStock/Getty Images Plus.

The following image is sourced from another image library: p. 60: Adrian Sherratt/Alamy Stock Photo

Front cover photography by irin-k, Lipowski Milan, Nella, photomatz, Polina Katritch, PowerUp, Olga Utchenko, Kazantseva Olga, Dirk Ercken, Maria Uspenskaya.

Designer: Chefer

The authors and publishers would like to thank the following illustrators:

Illustrations by Gaby Zermeño: pp. 4, 6-7, 9, 11, 13, 15, 17, 18-19, 23, 25, 27-29, 30-31, 33, 35, 37, 41, 42-43, 45, 47, 49, 51, 53, 54-55, 57-59, 61, 65-67, 69-70, 73, 75, 77, 90-95; Tim Bradford: pp. 8, 10-13, 14, 15-17, 20, 22, 24, 26, 28, 32, 34, 36, 39, 40, 46, 48, 50, 52, 58, 62, 64, 68, 70, 72, 74, 76-79, 81, 82, 85-88; Antonio Cuesta p. 9.

Unit 1

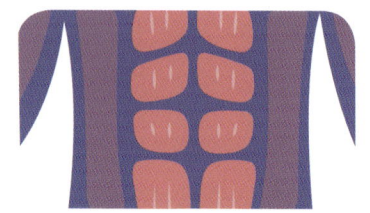 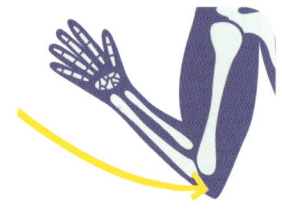

Unit 2

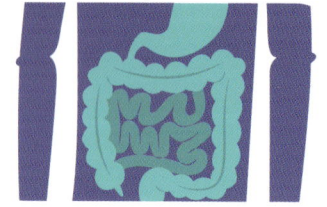 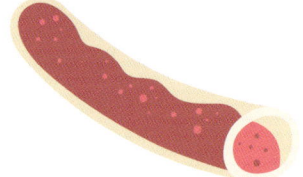 

Unit 3

Unit 4

Unit 5

Unit 6